In all this world, with all its possibilities for connections and
disconnections, what arrangement
of events can have occurred, to bring about the arrival
at one time and one place, the people on this
particular lonely coast?

Visions

NEIL STANNERS

Published by Garamonde 2019

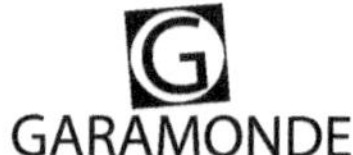

International distribution.
Copyright (Text and Covers) Neil Stanners 2019
The moral right of the author has been asserted.

ISBN 978-1-86275-013-5

Production by Media Services

Neil Stanners was born in Sydney.

He lived and worked in Europe.

He now resides once again in Sydney.

CHAPTERS

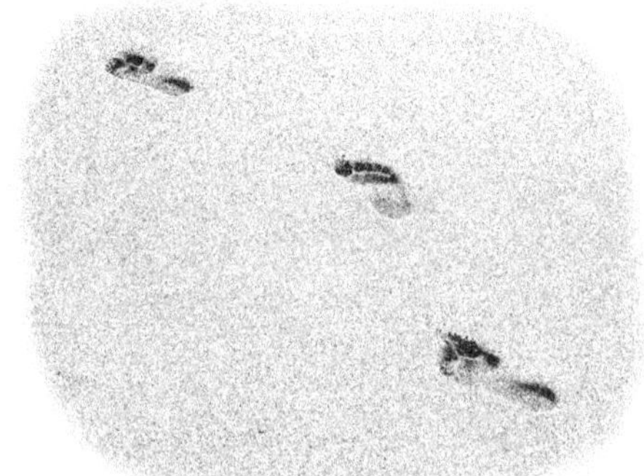

Sand

Sand is mellifluous. It sings through your fingers and squeaks under your feet. It calls on the wind to rattle against the world. It holds back the ocean to suck the life from a wave, so that the power within its depths is subdued and retreats.

Sand is a granular material that occurs naturally. It consists of finely divided rock and mineral particles. Largely composed of silica, sand can vary greatly in composition depending on the local materials that complete its composition.

In ocean environments the common form of sand is calcium carbonate. It has been created over millions of years by the breaking down of all types of shellfish and coral.So the components are primarily quartz, igneous rock, shell fragments and chert.

Geologists recognise sand particles as having a diameter between 0.0625 mm to 2 mm.

Wet sand is particularly difficult to remove from inside swimwear and between toes.

Sunlight

It is the essence of life. It is life. It wakes us in the morning and leaves us for the night.

We see, we feel, we dwell within its presence.

It warms us, grows our food, paints perfect pictures with a subtlety or exuberance we cannot master.

It watches us grow and knows our every move.

It toasts us in our play and burns us if we play too long.

It is our master and our lover.

Daylight is our visible section of the electromagnetic spectrum. It is the portion of radiation between infrared and ultraviolet given off by the Sun. Direct solar radiation is experienced as sunshine. Diffused sunlight is that which is reflected off other objects or has passed through clouds. Earthly sunlight is filtered through the planet's atmosphere. When the sun is above the horizon sunlight is everywhere as daylight. Sunlight is a key factor in photosynthesis, a process vital for living beings on Earth. Sunlight assists in knowing our friends, seeing our lovers and noticing our enemies.

Without it we could be blind to all three.

The sunlight here is like no other. It drenches those within it's scope in a brightness that opens up every pore in skin, the weave in cloth, the intricacies of a leaf or the back of a beetle. It leaves no doubt, nowhere to hide. It owns the landscape. It is the judge and the jury.

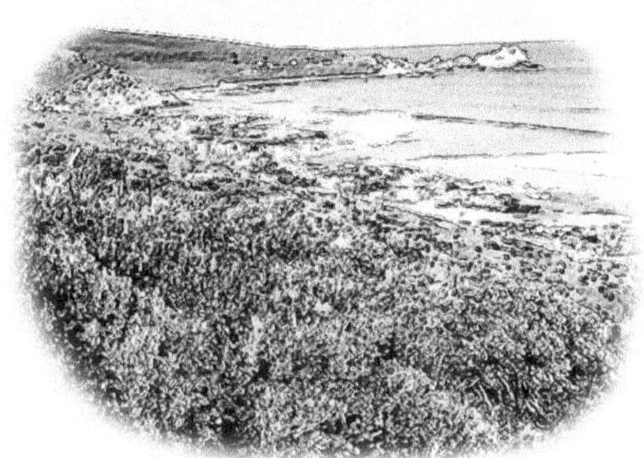

Coastal Heath

There was a girl who loved a boy called Heath. He was a handsome, likeable lad of fine disposition. She confessed to her friends she would like to romp with Heath in the heath. They told Heath. He thought it a wonderful idea for it seemed he secretly admired his admirer. The girl of course was mortified that her secret had been revealed and never spoke of Heath again.

Heath is also a city. It sits on oceanside hills and slopes. Combed by the wind like a fine Dandy's hair it protects a world of birds, reptiles, marsupials and such like and even gives refuge to the occasional interloper.
Heaths are rarely more than two metres tall, generally a lot less. They grow where conditions are warm and dry, particularly in summer. Heath lives in often sandy, acidic soils of low fertility. Heath vegetation is extremely plant-species rich. Bountiful in a way. The heathlands of Australia are home to approximately 3,700 endemic or typical species. Australian heathland is dominated by nectar feeding birds such as Honey-eaters and Lorikeets although numerous other birds are common. Australian heathlands are also home to the world's only nectar feeding terrestrial mammal: the Honey Possum.
Heaths are a great place to play the hide and seek game of 'Now You See Us Now You Don't.'

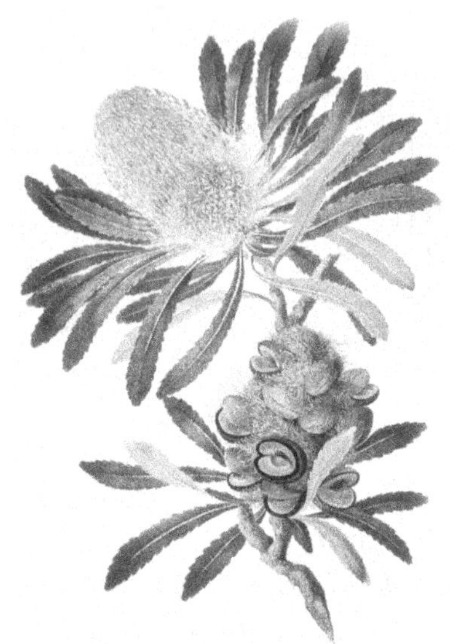

Banksia

They're evil. Any child who grew up in Australia and read books or had them read at bedtime knows the stories. No matter how grown up you become, no matter how sophisticated, you cannot pass a Banksia tree without a sidelong glance.

Banksias live and grow on the Australian east coast. They are generally a low shrub in coastal heath but can grow to eight metres tall. They have wrinkled bark and dark green serrated leaves large yellow flower heads. The flower's spikes turn grey as they age and large grey follicles appear. Banksia resprouts from its woody lignotuber after bushfires. Many mammals, birds, and invertebrates visit the inflorescences and aid pollination.

When dried out the large banksia seed pods with their evil eyes and mouths are excellent for the scaring of small children by older children.

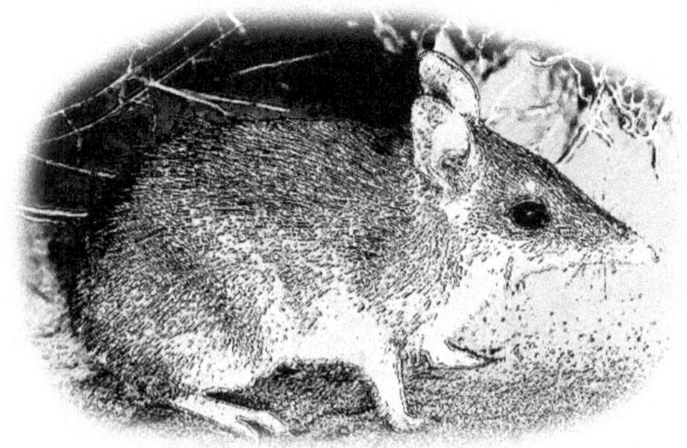

Bandicoots

They are small and very cute.
About the size of a half grown cat.
What are those puzzling conical holes in the lawn.
Good stuff down there. Worms, insects, tubers, roots, fungi.
At a distance they are sometimes mistaken for rodents
Bandicoots are omnivorous marsupials. They are found
throughout Australia. There are a few different species.
Bandicoots can live in a wide variety of habitats, from
rainforests to wet and dry woodlands to heathland.
They mainly forage at night. Careful where you step.

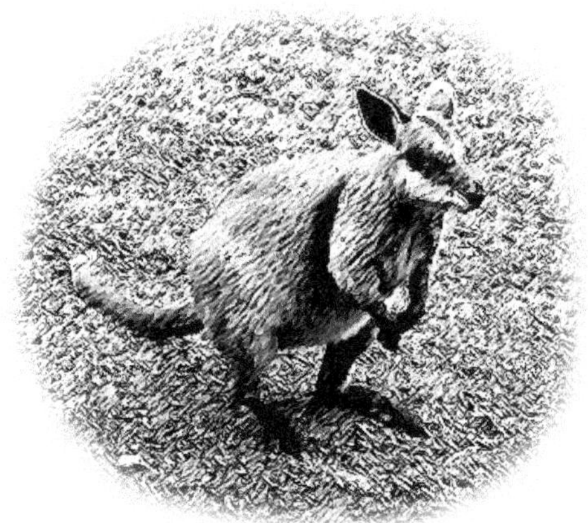

Swamp Wallaby (Black Wallaby)

*Perhaps because they're fluffy and have that black muzzle
you can find no people who have a dislike for the swamp
wallaby. Could it be that they always look a little
concerned about the world?*

*They're solitary, and at best about waist high. Apart from
their habit of leaving it until you've almost walked into
them before hopping away they have no irritating traits.
And they have long eyelashes. They're pretty.*

*This wallaby is also commonly known as the black
wallaby. They are found down the entire east coast of
Australia. Their gait differs from other wallabies.
The swamp wallaby carries its head low and tail out
straight.*

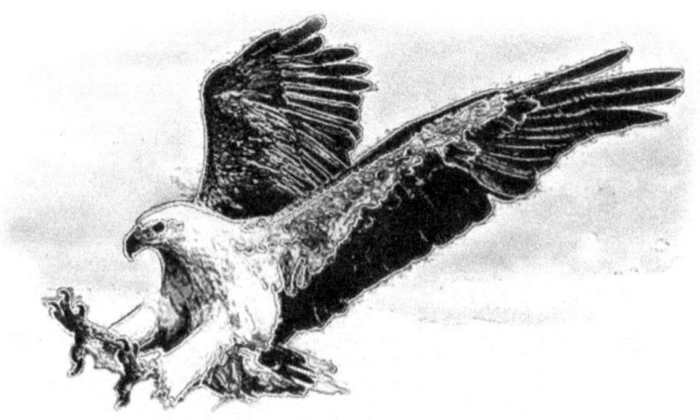

White Sea Eagle

They're up there, watching you. Silent, like a ghost in the sky. Huge with keen eyes and a wicked beak. Puff yourself up. Make it understood that you're too big to be carried off back to their nest.

The spectacular Australian White-bellied Sea-Eagle is similar in shape to the well-known Wedge-tailed Eagle and almost as large. It is distinguished by its contrasting crisp-white and ashy-grey plumage.

The wingspan is about 1.8 m - 2 m.

White-bellied Sea-Eagles are normally seen perched high in a tree, or soaring over waterways and adjacent land. The birds form permanent pairs that inhabit territories throughout the year.

The White-bellied Sea-Eagle feeds mainly off aquatic animals, such as fish, turtles and sea snakes, but it takes birds and mammals as well.

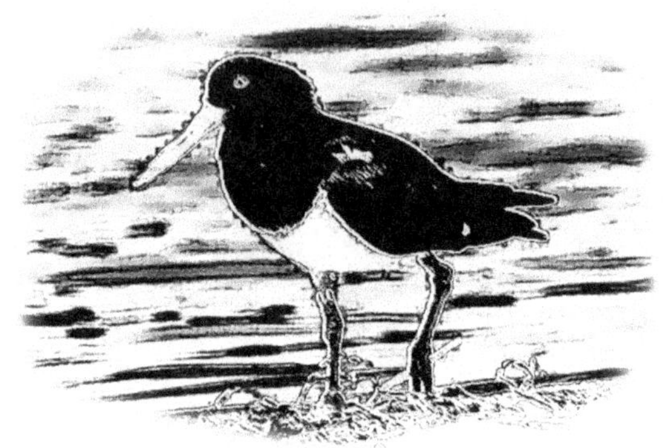

Sooty Oystercatcher

*They are there, in the corner of your eye. Now there, now
gone. A head, you think you saw. Perhaps you're sitting
on rocks at the end of a beach. Watching the waves,
admiring their fluency. You are being observed?*
Don't look back to the waves. Watch the rocks.
The collection of scattered rocks with sand between.
With each wave washing through them.
And suddenly this comic mate appears for you.
*Poking about, exploring, like an old man with plenty of
time and the faint belief that treasure may lie nearby.*
That curious black head, the bright red pointed beak.
*It is the eye that makes the connection. Black and beady,
surrounded by that same red.*
*Each time the head comes up, "Hullo," "Hi, still here,"
"No, nothing yet. Nice day though," "Still there I see.
Just sitting eh," "Ooops found something." "Hullo again,
doing alright here."*
*The Sooty Oystercatcher can be found right round the
Australian coast. They never stray far from beaches and
estuaries. Apart from their red eyes, legs and beak they
are all black. Their call is a double 'per-peep.'*

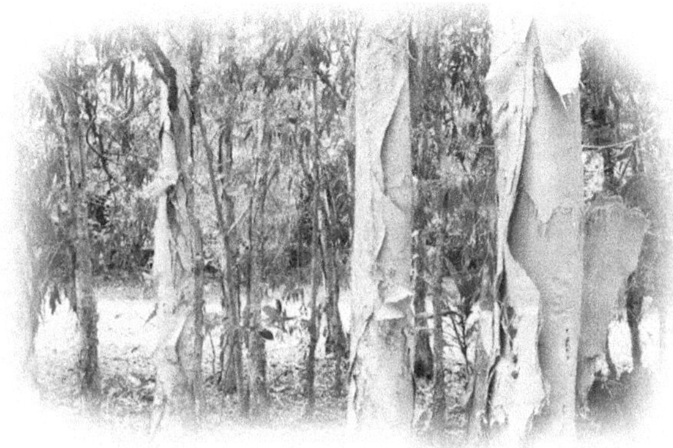

Paperbarks

How can a tree have bark like paper. Well, it does.
They're magic, somehow. Ask a cornstalk.
Many trees have been stripped a little too harshly by some
game that involved collecting sheets of the bark.
It can be written on with difficulty.
Add enough imagination and it's paper. It's soft too.
Not hard or harsh or scratchy like many other trees.
Just soft ..... like paper.

The Paperbark grows on the Australian east coast from
the tropics well down into the sub-temperate regions.
They can grow to between 7 and 14 metres so they are not
a large tree. They can happily handle water and can grow
freely in swampy land. They have narrow dark green
leaves. Their flowering is quite prolific producing masses
of fluffy white flowers. An even bigger Paperbark grows in
the tropics.

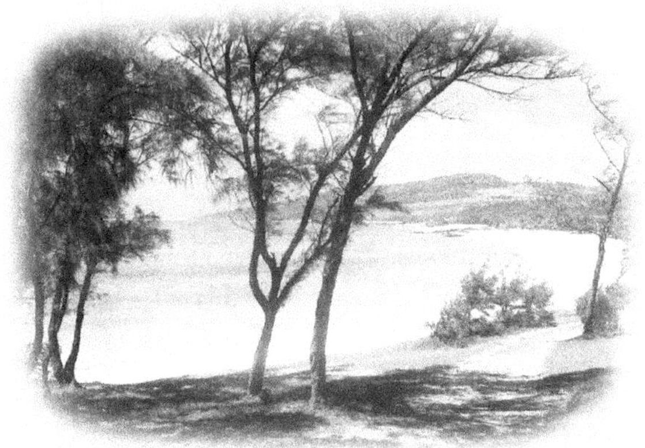

Sheoaks

*People seem to only have pleasant memories of these
trees. Sheoaks are those large trees with thousands of fine
tendrils, instead of leaves. Imagine long pine needles.
They grow by rivers and streams, on coastal beaches
and in the mountains. Places where people have good
times. They sway and move in gentle wafts of their dense
green bodies. At night they sing you to sleep as the breeze
brushes through their foliage. The sound is like that of a
soothing mother shooshing her baby to rest.*
*Their foliage drops and forms soft, spongy ground beneath
their branches. This in turn absorbs sound. It's very quiet
near sheoaks. (Except when there's a breeze.)*

*The Casuarina has seventeen sub-species. The biggest can
grow to thirty-five metres tall. They produce hard woody
'fruit' like small, solid pine cones.*
Wood turners love the timber.

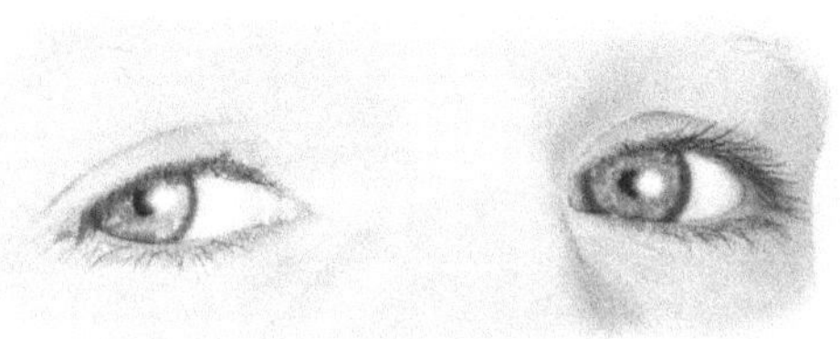

Australian Child

In the early days they were known as 'cornstalks.'
The children of the colony grew straight and true under
the sun. Their food was fresh, their spirits unfettered.
They were golden and clear faced. Activity and clean air
made them strong.
Adults newly arrived compared them with the pale,
wasted children of Europe and named them after the corn
that grew straight and strong in the fields, seeking the sun.

And years and decades and a century passed and they are
as they were. When you find some cornstalks today they
are all those things and perhaps a little more. The land-
scape has invaded their being. It is not in all but you'll
know the ones when you see them. There's something
there. Intangible, a confidence, a knowledge, a presence,
who can say.

But you'll know. It's in their eyes.

CHAPTER 1

Changes

Imagine that you are a bird. A seabird. One that nests on cliffs above a restless ocean. Your wings are large and on the pillow of air that folds up and over your nesting place, you can with little effort, hold a position for hours. In odd flexes and tilts of your body, you can position yourself up and down the sheer wall of rock that drops away to smashing white water below. With a keen eye, there is little that passes beneath that you do not see.

Today, however, the sea is calm. It rolls about in a green pulse like a half-set jelly. You note the sliced edge of the cliff, the soft line of grass at the top, striated beige and white lines in the rock's face.

A path winds doodling up from the distant pale yellow beach and then parallels the cliff edge. It is a hiker's path, though rarely used in this remote world. It withers near the

highest point and for those who care to look there is another
path, it's beginnings hidden by a bent, torn old tree. It runs
away from the lands extremity down into a stand of timber.
They are paperbarks. Growing in a mysterious mini forest,
enjoying the moist soil. All this is within your realm as you
float in the light of early morning.

Your head flicks as you detect a new movement. On the
path, coming up and away from the beach, there is a child.
She represents nothing that is of benefit to a lofty seabird.
She runs, her arms outstretched, fingers groping and feeling
the air. She is barefoot, covered in a filmy, flimsy, flickering
reflecting material. On her back are two inadequate wings
of the same material. They are stretched out in the same
manner as her arms. Moving loosely about in the breeze.
At the summit, by the bent tree, she stops. With a delicate
child finger, she slides back her long hair, up and behind her
ear.
Then she is away again, tripping and skipping down the
grassy line away from the cliff edge.
Rising a little you can watch casually as the girl reaches the
open flat area that precedes the trees. Her feet are wet from
the muddy drainage of the soft soil. With purpose, at a hurry,
free from the wind, she moves on lightly and enters the
trees, then she is gone.

CHAPTER 2

It Begins

A high-powered bruiser of a wind turned up an hour after they went to bed. It then buffeted the cottage walls throughout the night, pausing only briefly to adjust its attack.

In the single large bedroom, Jennifer briefly lay a hand on the chest of her husband. He still excited her. The man slept in the deep halls of exhaustion and presented no potential for the woman's interest.

Ill at ease, she drifted into a fitful sleep.

Doors moved, walls sighed, the roof at times indicated imminent departure. In her waking moments, Jennifer considered the wisdom of arriving after midnight.

This place was unknown and isolated, well away from the highway or a town. It's delightful, peaceful and free.

The information from fleeting family recollections.

She could hear the surf and that pleased her. It boomed then lulled rolling over the rock-face below the house. It filled her mind with childish memories. Silly secrets from a vague past. Away at the other side of the house, the children lay together on a double bed in an enclosed verandah.
Each feigned sleep.
Their thoughts reflected their ages.
Liz lay still. Relaxed, she thought of the six weeks holiday ahead and was only slightly annoyed that her legs protruded from the end of the inadequate little sheet that covered them.
Marty imagined a war zone. It helped dull his concern about the roof.
Denny was the least convincing. His eyes kept jumping open. Each creak and gust had them searching the darkness in a new direction.
All three knew they would have no sleep this night.

Simultaneously, possibly because Marty gave one of his elaborate twitches, they woke to an impossibly bright, hot room. A beam of gold so thick and intense that it could surely be cut in slices, came through the window and burned a sharp rectangle on the door of the wardrobe.
Each wet child, stuck with sweat, groaned and moved on the bed, waking and stirring, trying to remember where they were.
Beyond the windows of the verandah, they could see blue. Because of the oddness of the house and the small headland they occupied they could make out both sky and sea. So overwhelming, these hues coloured the sand and grasses of

the headland.

"Impressive eh?"
Tom Brandy, their Dad. The one, the only 'Tomdad', stood in
the doorway supping cereal from a bowl.
Liz reached him first. She silently clawed the gold hair of his
arm in a ritual of excitement, grinned up at him then headed
through the house to the breakfast table. Tomdad followed
after accepting similar feelings of gratitude from his two
sons.

Jenny fed them bowls of cut fruit. It ran down chins and
chests and they laughed and were silly. She didn't care.
This was not a tidy house.
"The water tastes weird," said Liz, looking scientifically at
her glass.
"It's from a tank, my dear." Jenny looked at her daughter.
"No chemicals."
"Just bugs," added Tom.
"Thanks for your support."
He changed the subject. Though the children were
apparently oblivious.
"Dibs on the front box room. Now I know where the sun
comes in. God, you could roast a chicken in the kid's
verandah." Tomdad touched his son's shoulder, still hot from
sleep.
"We'll work something out. I'm going to take my painting
gear and go in search of Egrets. Do some roughs. Take some
photos. Always sell Egrets. People just love 'em."
"Big, Little or Intermediate?" Marty asked, with a sideways
glance.

Tomdad put his son in a headlock. "I know you're being a smartarse but it shows you listen. So good for that. Anybody want to come?"

"Fine then," he said after a fair length of silence.

"Wouldn't just a camera be easier?" Jenny enquired.

"You can cheat and draw them up back here. It's not cheating if they're your photos."

Tom looked at his wife. "How long have you known me? Nothing like some plein-air studies to get the feel. But yeh, I'll take photos and do all the hard slog here with some wine and crackers and my lovely family nearby."

Morning moved on sliding into day. It warmed, even more, producing a drugged, empty landscape. Nothing in the touch of the morning kingdom moved.

The Brandy children, not cognisant of nature's wishes, dragged their parents about the house and its general area in order to examine all possible aspects of their new environment.

Jenny viewed the clutch from behind smiling appropriately when encouraged by their enthusiasm. Tom, except perhaps for his greater height could easily have been a child.

They danced from odd bushes hiding a bird's nest, to the beginnings of the sand dunes with the footprints of a gecko in a continuing row of 'S' shapes.

They ran, rolled and laughed. Jenny smiled at their antics. She joined in some but preferred to observe.

They lay on the grass and stared into the sky. A row of bodies. Their clothes had all but vanished following their arrival. Just shorts, never more.

"What do you see?" Tom waited.

"Blue."

"I see blue."

"Yep, blue."

He cuffed their ears. "What do you see?"

"Okay," said Marty, "I'm taking a closer look here now."

"I see a pool. There are blue fish just below the surface. They're slow because the water is warm."

"Oh yes." Denny pinched his brother's arm with excitement. "I have a blue net, so the fish won't see it coming."

"You're supposed to have original thoughts." Marty bared his teeth at his little brother.

Jennifer looked at Liz. She lay still, her eyes fixed on the sky.

"Liz?" prompted Jennifer.

"I see infinity."

Tom picked up his daughter's hand and kissed it.

"And what is at the end?"

She turned her head and stared into her father's eyes.

"More infinity," she whispered."Did I get the benign smile right?" Liz queried as they stood.

"You always do child. My little mystery. Some man someday will be very bewildered by knowing you."

Walking back to the house they were subdued. Jennifer laid down a rule for their stay. It involved appearing at mealtimes. It became the only rule. Within an hour she was alone in the house.

The following day with the confidence and knowledge of their first day's exploration they were all gone by eight. When she realised she was alone once more Jenny gave a short laugh, rubbing her neck, stretching. It was as it was.

She spoke to herself, to the air, to the void.

"Seriously," she said, "what did you expect?"

CHAPTER 3

Finding Things

From the bleached wood walls of the house, a slight track
leads away over the low headland heading south.
It follows the curve of the wide sandstone promontory,
through thick coastal heath. Melaleucas and dwarfed
banksias which grow to about knee height and lay away from
the ocean breeze as if stroked by a giant's hand.
While their father hurried off to the north, packed with a
camera, sketch pad and watercolours in search of birds,
the children followed the track south. Around their low
headland, it climbed and finally dropped and then split at
the base of a deeply inset high straight cliff. To the right a
climb up along the rim of the cliffs disappearing from view.
To the left and only a few short steps down from their feet
lay a huge flat beach.
It looked like a private amphitheatre. The children

involuntarily glanced up as if expecting an audience.

This was new territory.

Marty expressed the group sentiment. "Wow," he said quietly.

Mottled by some broken clouds it lay, like a stage, awaiting their performance. No crowd to hiss a bad line, no humans at all. In the still air the emptiness excited them. They had taken possession of a part of the world and it was their's alone.

"What have you been doing?" Jennifer asked at the obligatory lunch check-in. She had several books alongside the lounge on the balcony. In the centre of an old uncertain table, dragged from indoors, a wet cloth covered sandwiches and fruit in bowls.

There passed a conspiratorial smile among her children. The beach was a treasure to be guarded. They deflected the question with vague references to walking, swimming and exploring.

"Swimming, I might join you. A swim would be nice."

"It's a long way." Denny looked up from his sandwich. "You should use the little beach out the front."

"Where's Dad?" Liz rolled her eyes at Denny as she spoke.

Their mother sighed. "Broken the rule. Took his lunch. God knows where he's gone."

She sounded a little annoyed.

"Dad's in trou .. ble," mumbled Denny, his head down and mouth full of sandwich.

Liz rolled her eyes at her younger brother yet again.

As the children departed, hurrying to avoid the possibility

of their mother insisting on joining them, Marty could not resist an enquiry.

"You came here when you were young. Don't you remember anything?"

"I was five," she replied, with a wan smile. "I remember fish. Flopping about when they were landed on the rocks, knives going into their white bellies to gut them and the endless meals of fish. Grandpa once said, 'that's a superb king.' It took several years before I found out that the big red fish with the bulbous head-crown, was what he was talking about. I think I swam somewhere. The waves scared me. And I started a shell collection. That completes my knowledge of my childhood here. We stopped coming. My Grandad and my father had a falling out. Sulked for years and didn't speak to each other. I think this house and land being left to my father and then in turn left to me was some minor act of contrition on everybody's part. Dad only came here occasionally to fix the place up when he got it. No more family visits."

"What's contrition?" asked Denny.

"Sort of feeling sorry for something you did."

"So are there any other houses around here?" Marty asked, as he was surreptitiously pulled toward the steps by his sister.

Jennifer Brandy looked with too much interest at the threesome.

"Not that I know. The national park seems to have cut off any plans for this part of the coast. Why?"

They were away, running off toward their track.

"Take care of each other," she called, and as an odd afterthought, floating in the air, aimed at their disappearing backs, aware of their unconventional upbringing, "And keep your clothes on."

They had beach clothes and towels but she knew they'd just swim in their shorts and dry in the sun. At least she hoped they'd stay in their shorts.

Jennifer stood for some time looking at the empty track. It went out of focus. She blinked at the realisation.

Moving inside she touched the door-jamb then the scarred walls, running her hand across memories that she did not completely own. Each dent no doubt represented some point in a life spent here all those years ago. Perhaps boisterous play by children or a fishing rod swung too hard going down the corridor.

There were ghosts of people seated at the kitchen table, laying sleeping on the lounge chair, draped at the windows quietly viewing the ocean.

She sighed, surprised again at her melancholy mood. In all the times of her life that filed into her character, including the early childhood at this place, she had very little memory of her mother. A woman who moved in and out of her life with such fatal regularity that in the end, Jennifer accepted the comings and goings as normality.

Perhaps the last time she saw her grandfather held more answers than she imagined.

She had awoken to raised voices at their home. Her older sister in the other bed slept on but she had slipped down the hallway and sat on the cold boards while her grandfather and father discussed things she did not understand. The words 'slut' and 'tramp' had been used in relation to her mother. Her mother who was 'away' again. It was the last

time she ever saw her grandfather and the second last time
she ever saw her mother.

Years later at her grandfather's graveside, she looked at his
dark coffin and thought of the hurtful words. As the man
of religion had made a ritual of the occasion with talk and
gestures, she whispered to her father, "When are we going to
the cottage?"

"Never," he replied, "he can't make up for it all from beyond."
They never did go. When their father left it to his daughters,
Miranda had looked at the Will and said, "I'll take my share
of the money Sis. The cottage is yours. Don't want to know
about it. All bad. Burn it down. I don't care."

Miranda had inherited that first child pragmatism that is so
sensible and so little fun.

Her Dad, had little time for most things in his later years. He
didn't like Tom. "The fella's a dreamer."

Practicality and purpose. It left no room for quality. Life was
to be managed. He did it well. He made quite a lot of money
in his small boating business but never kept employees long.
He loved his grandchildren but seemed scared of them. Left
them scholarships to a good school.

Jennifer knew he left the earth a rather sad, disillusioned
man. She carried a guilt that she could not have done
something to put a small spark back into his being.

He had been gone over a year. Tom knew they had the
house. He did not mention it. She loved him for that. Tom
was big on time being an unappreciated medicine. When she
had announced a few weeks ago at the dinner table that they
were going to take a long drive to their cottage by the sea,

the children had been incredulous.

"We have a cottage?" "Since when?" "Where?" "What sea?" "Holy cow!"

After the initial surprise, they did the children thing of simple acceptance. Okay, we have a cottage. That's good. Marty's sudden need for a little more detail had caught her off guard. She suspected Tom had been filling in a few more basic facts while trying ineptly to remain vague.

CHAPTER 4

The First Meeting

Their father Tom had explanatory names for most of the objects, situations and events in their lives. The children had yet to decide whether it was a form of fatherly goodwill constructed to make life understandable for his offspring or his own attempt at coming to terms with his world. Or perhaps he had 'loose thoughts' as one visiting schoolfriend had put it. She had been overheard. Their Dad said how much he liked the term but Violet French had gone bright red and had never returned.

Right now, today, they were dealing with a 'lazy surf.' Distantly, with no impact on their position, it limped ashore as if their mother's cornflour had been added as a thickening agent.

"I think the surf's fat," Denny offered.

"No, lazy is better." Marty gave his little brother a half-smile for effort then slipped into the coming wave. The water was cold. A shaking, shocking brief cold before his hot body adjusted. The water was warm now.

An hour later the day had heated and dried the salt on their skin. The sun developed a bite.
In the whole expanse of this very wide, almost flat beach, they were the sole inhabitants. It had green frilly edges of lush vegetation and the surrounding cliffs provided some black patches of shade but overall the beach was open and hot. They had taken up a position somewhere in the middle where the sand held some moisture.
The hole they had dug was extensive. Surrounded by a wall of excavated sand it had a flat base with sufficient room for all three of its occupants to lounge about in relative comfort. This particular sand had a quality that allowed it to stay bound and thus their walls were almost vertical. Eventually, it would fill with water when the tide returned across the wide, open expanse that only gained some height when it approached the beach grass and rocks near the base of the cliffs. It most definitely had a theatrical feel as if something was about to happen once the silent overture was complete.

"Dad would have said we were 'possessed by the idea."
Liz stroked her little brother's hair. His head resting on her stomach. He was proud of his memory.
Marty played his toes against his sister's. It was all he could manage. Digging the hole had come to them collectively. Despite their youth, they were temporarily enfeebled. Now completed to their satisfaction the hole was so deep that Liz and Marty could only just see over the top when standing.

At the bottom of their hole they let the sun sweep over them.
Clouds interrupted the heat periodically. A dark hand
moving across the landscape. The wet sand cooled, then the
sun broke free and sought them out again.
Denny had been worried.
"How will we get out?"
"The same way we got in," said Liz, "we'll dig."
"Or if the tide comes in, we'll just swim out," added Marty.

Infrequently but with some feeling of necessity, Marty would
roll onto his stomach and then his knees then up to his feet
to peer over their battlements to report nothing.
Finally, after many checks, he was able to give some minor
news.
"Uh, somebody in the distance."
A speck, a black stick figure moved along at the top of the
hill. Hard to distinguish in the glare against the dark green
wind-washed bush on the slope.
They soon lost interest.
Denny attacked Liz with a handful of wet sand and received
an overwhelming response.
It left him sputtering. In pity, she then had to take him in
her arms and spend some time brushing away the evidence
of her assault and clearing his eyes. She blew gently on the
nape of his neck for the fun of watching him shudder.
Marty was indifferent, legs tangled again with his sister's.
Lumped against the side of the hole he was tiring of their
occupation and gaining in hunger. He looked at his empty
stomach hanging out of his shorts. It lay flat. In considerable
need of topping up. His eyes flickered, almost asleep.
A shadow appeared on his skin. A round shadow.

"Oh, so sorry."

Marty glanced up.

From their languid positions, the children looked to the source of the voice. Difficult to see more than an outline. The ball of the sun sat directly behind the speaker. He was a Kurdaitcha man, the Koori dream figure from cave walls. Their eyes fought to create a tangible image.

"I wondered what this big lump was in the middle of my beach? Didn't know it was inhabited. Quite a job you've done, though. Quite a job."

He hovered, looking down at them, moving slightly, now visible. Bolts of sunlight cut past as he shifted and lit their bodies like rifle shots. This man with a short cut beard seemed reluctant to leave but the children's idleness gave him no opening to delay.

"Sorry, to disturb you."

He was gone.

Liz looked at Denny then up again. She smiled. "Just a man." She kissed her little brother.

"My beach? Did you hear that?" Marty worked on his incredulity.

Denny looked up at Liz and touched her face. "Were you worried?"

"No," she said, "just a man."

At the evening meal, there seemed to be stiffness about proceedings. The children realised that Tom was in trouble for disappearing all day. They could not know that the concerns of their mother in returning to the cottage were rather brittle and Tom might well have been advised to stay close-by for a few days in order to lend silent moral support.

He realised all this now as they ate a quite elaborate meal.
The cottage at least had electricity and an amazing old
refrigerator built in the days when such household items
never died. The building had cooled considerably by letting
the ocean breezes flow through from front to back.
Gazpacho, spicy cold chicken, aioli, garden salad with
croutons and ever onward. Jenny had kept busy by working
in the kitchen. They ate quietly until they could eat no more.
Late in the evening with the children sleeping off that
glorious exhaustion of childhood, Tom tried to explain his
insensitivity by boyish excitement and an overwhelming
urge to rush out and explore.
Lying beside her husband in the darkness Jenny could not
help but be won over by his entreaties and the strange
knowledge that, buried in his attempts at humour, lay a
kernel of truth. He was what he was. The nicest person she
could ever possibly meet. She smiled secretly and put a
hand on his chest.
They made love quietly for an hour then fell into a deep
sleep.

Notebook of Leo Cassems
January 5
*I am stunned. I have a picture, framed and round. A
circumference of sand. Three children in a hole on my beach.
Perhaps it was the light. Could have been my mood or theirs?
Heat does warp things, mind, body, sight. Walking today.*

Idling, yes idling. Vacantly pursuing thoughts. What Georgie said in the New Year phone call. Reclusive, uninspired. Mulling over it all. There in the centre of the sand is a biggish hole. Have to investigate. Turtle maybe? Bloody big one. Obviously too big for an animal. What?

Approached it with the assumption that it would be shallow and empty but it's quite deep and straight-sided. There in the bottom, mixed together, tangled, sweating, spotlighted by the sun overhead were three quite beautiful creatures. Girl, boy and younger boy. Light brown skin, green uncanny eyes, something soft and melancholy about them. Greek tragedy in form. Incredible limbs, flawless skin, an air of 'indifference'? Don't kids jump when surprised? Aren't strangers potentially hostile?

Their hair was slightly sun-bleached. Outdoors kids.

I wanted to be sure they weren't just brats in a good light but by God, I was looking at them in intense light. The sort that cuts to the deepest flaw and exposes it to the world. With them, there was nothing, as they shifted trying to see me against the sun. I can see them on canvas. It is a sincere vision. Feel the colours that will hold them. Produce something of that moment. I feel a challenge has been made. Only now I don't understand what happened. They, these little humans, made me uncomfortable. It was their manner.

Now, the dilemma. Do I work from memory and botch the whole thing or do I approach them again and have the 'vision' confirmed or denied? In another time and another place, will they prove to be just irksome and imperfect?

It was the mood of the occasion as much as the image.

The Diary of Elizabeth Brandy

January 5

Our beach is lovely. We can do anything at our beach. The cliffs watch us from three sides and the other side is the ocean. We raced some dolphins through the waves. They won. Maybe we can perform a play with the cliffs as an audience. A man came. I think he was curious about our hole. Tomorrow we'll look north.

CHAPTER 5

The Second Meeting

From the cliff, the beach looked as it always did. A flat
expanse of yellow/white with a slash of ultramarine blue
providing a line of separation to the bleached blue sky.
Yesterday the beach had remained empty except for the
brief appearance and disappearance of two people with
backpacks, struggling across the sand and heading away to
the south.
The tide had visited the hole and gently flattened it to a dish.
Little more than an indication of the previous excavation.
Leo Cassems waited on the clifftop at various times
throughout the hot day. Each time breasting the last line
of rocks, bringing the beach into view. Each time excited
at the prospect of seeing figures, once more inhabiting this
domain. Each time becoming increasingly morose at their
non-appearance.

By day's end, the man, whose moods and passions produced his work, had them turn against him. He sat throughout the evening drinking claret from a cask. Angry at his helplessness. He felt also slightly afraid. His paintings were a rich mix of land and the circumstance of people. He had always followed notions, no matter how irrational because he knew they were manifestations of his creativity. Invariably they carried him through and in doing so reassured him and made him bolder, able to confidently push new boundaries of image. To capture human interface with the world in ways that shocked and quite surprised those that took art seriously. His art was dark. It contained black and shadows. By contrast, the bright sections where light intruded drew the viewer into the work. It was Cassems' style. Recognisable images but strengthened and moulded to bold imaginings holding viewers with their mystery. A reinterpreted world.

Now, alone and drunk, he quietly cursed his curiosity. A tree or a rock, seen and admired, remained static and available. His mind noted things and he eventually revisited them, to sketch or possibly photograph. Even the fairly rare people in his art were easily accessible. The humans or creatures in his art were always a construct of memory, akin to stage props for the greater good of the entire work.
This new problem was one of interaction with unknown humans. He enjoyed solitude. He was not especially good at dealing with people. Not through a shyness but a need to be selfish. The women in his life passed through like travellers. Ignored until needed they had all simply kissed him goodbye, and smiled as they moved away. Often he hardly noticed.

The next morning he slept late. Once awake he hurried
to the beach annoyed at his eagerness. A full tide made it
smaller. A strong surf rolled in. Quite perfect waves.
And nobody to enjoy them. He sat for some time staring into
the distant water the way a camper watches a fire.
When he first moved to this headland, remote and pressed
against a national park, he often swam. Georgie, his agent,
would conjure up bizarre headlines featuring the search for
or recovery of his body. The shark that had taken him away.
Danger, isolation and the sheer crispness of water and waves
'rinsed his brain' he would tell her.
There was a woman at that time. For a while, he swam
and they had quite insane sex in more and more elaborate
places. Trying to paint her was a frustrating exercise. Her
body became awkward on the canvas. He tried softer media,
pastels and washing about in gouache until he realised that
he did not like her and she irritated him. Then she was gone
and he rediscovered lichen on rocks, gullies with ferns, trees
with a character that held a lifetime in their gnarled trunks
and he was at peace.

In the afternoon, convinced the children had gone, returned
to whatever town they had briefly left, he made one more
trip to the headland loathing his foolishness and swearing
it would be his last. The tide was out, the sun high. It hurt
the eyes to squint across the sand and the bright reflected
shine from the beach. In the middle, like some magical worm
home, was a freshly created hole.
For minutes, his heart racing, Leo Cassems stood, watching
this one spot of the beach. The image began to oscillate.

He squeezed his eyes a number of times. Nothing moved.
Nothing changed. Were they in residence? Was it some
others who had moved in?
Faintly, through the haze, he picked up movement. The two
boys emerged from the surf. The older one helping the small
one until they cleared the white water. They ran to the hole
and launched themselves into it in a joint, conspiratorial
dive. Cassems thought he heard a squeal of protest.
Then silence. He took a solid breath. Now he would know.

When almost at the hole the artist convinced himself not to
proceed. 'How awkward,' he thought. Predatorial. Perhaps
a wrong impression. Sneaking up on them. Curiosity pulled
him across the final small distance to the lip of the hole.
That and the silence.

They lay in each other's arms. A complex collection of
limbs. Their eyes were closed. Possibly exhaustion from
their ceaseless activity. Each held the other loosely. Cassems
was presented with another 'image', so still and so beautiful
that he thought immediately of death. He remonstrated with
himself for making such a mental connection. They were his
this time. Unaware of his presence, they lay obediently, like
glassed-in specimens while he checked his memory of the
original encounter. Every essence of the previous snapshot
was there. Their fingers, limbs, the line of their jaws, the
elegant handsome faces. Even their skin had an odd almost
translucent quality. He felt exalted by the realisation that
his mind was correct. Absently he touched his baggy cargo
pants for the Conte pencil and small sketch pad he often
carried.

"Hullo". Cassems felt a shudder go through him. The girl had spoken. Those amazing eyes were open and looking at him. Otherwise she had not moved.

"You're back." Her voice was husky. It woke the others. Three sets of those eyes now roved over his face and locked on his own. No fear or suspicion. Such was their assuredness that none moved except to follow him with their eyes.

Not the apologetic sidelong glance of youth but a full steady gaze. He felt a moment of concern. Please don't let them ruin it. Don't be overbearing little products of some pretentious parental training.

Precocious he could not take.

"I'm a local here," he said, for no particular reason.

"I'm the only local in fact. We're neighbours. You have this magnificent hole and I have a house on the hill."

Cassems thought he saw a flicker of interest at the mention of his house. Perhaps they did not realise it was there, hidden beyond the cliffs. Still, they did not speak. He went on.

"You must have come from the town or are you camping out?" This elicited a response.

"No," the girl said, "we're at Grandpa's house over on the heathland."

It took a pause for Cassems to realise they were talking about a rundown old weatherboard building he had often visited in his first days here. He had notions that it may one day produce some people. He considered using it in a painting but decided it was a little too quaint.

"It was our Grandfather's. Now it's ours," the girl continued.

"He died," added the small boy, matter of factly.

"Yes," said the artist. "Well, my name is Leo Cassems.
You probably haven't heard of me but I'm a painter and live
up here and work out of the studio in my house."
The older boy spoke, still regarding him with that odd soft,
almost kindly look.
"We've heard of you. You're in some of Tomdad's books."

Notebook of Leo Cassems
January 7
*Why does life give answers that produce other questions? I
have met these children. I have talked with them and gained
some insight into their background, who they are and why
they suddenly appeared on my beach. They are wonderfully
strange. Everything I might have hoped for has been fulfilled.
Their organic otherworldly looks are nothing compared with
their characters. Immensely encouraged I have asked if I might
call and talk with their parents. Standing today looking at them
in their hole they could have grown from the sand, such was
their naturalness.*

*Now, of course, I am worried that this whole rush may be
nothing more than curiosity. Some sketches from memory
proved lifeless.*

*Their father, whom they refer to as 'Tomdad', is an artist with
the Natural History Museum. Could be awkward. I think I know
his work. Had some books of flora and fauna. Can't find them.
Sure he's in them.*

The Diary of Elizabeth Brandy

January 7

North of our house is boring. Heathland and cliffs. Lots of birds and little creatures for Tomdad. We found a tiny beach down the bottom of some cliffs. Denny got scared climbing down.

There was a cave but not very deep.

Today we went to our beach again. No dolphins.

Marty says that there are fish so small they can wait in a shell till the tide come back in. We couldn't find any.

We dug a new hole.

That man came back. He has a house somewhere behind the cliffs. He's famous. He's called Leo Cassems. He wants to come and visit us. Hope he's not going to claim 'his' beach back. He seems nice though. But I think he's shy.

CHAPTER 6

A Family Meeting

At 9.30 am the following day, Leo Cassems trimmed his
beard, showered, combed his hair back as best he could and
put on a clean white shirt. Upon reflection, he removed his
sandals and enclosed his feet in socks and boots. With dark
jeans and a leather belt, he was an imposing man. All black
hair and anger except that he had kindly eyes.

At the lowest point of the path as it begins to skirt the back
of the beach he realised that he had over-dressed. "I'll arrive
sweating and unpleasant," he conjectured. He made the rest
of the journey barefoot with his shirt off, praying that he did
not come upon these other people unexpectedly.
Near to the house but out of sight he wiped himself down
with the socks, thankful that he had a new pair. He smiled
briefly at the absurdity of the situation and then replaced

his white shirt and thus arrived at the screen door of the
weatherboard at 10 am, crumpled but calm.
Towels were draped about on the verandah railings.
Odd to see this building with small touches of habitation.
The towels were colourful but pleasant. They had none of
the crude inscriptions that adorn much of the standard
beach accoutrement. Cassems was oddly heartened by this.
If you can navigate through all the hideous offerings about
and find something that retains dignity then the world has a
purpose.
His gentle knock on the wooden screen door produced no
reaction. He realised for the first time that the house must
have a front door but the path led to the rear, oceanside
yard. Or a clearing of grass in the heath. He had naturally
crossed the verandah to the back door. On a table lay the
remains of a meal and a wine glass he noted.
The house, except for a fairly continual creaking and
adjusting to the day's sun, was without sound. He knocked
again. Somewhere inside, there came a movement. Down the
long corridor, lit from the rear by the morning sun entering
the house's large front windows, a figure appeared.
"Oh hullo, you must be Mr Cassems."
Leo Cassems said or thought, "Oh Christ."
He had given little thought to the parents. But of course,
the children's appearance had to have an origin. She walked
towards him, backlit and shining, drying her hair for God's
sake. Glowing soft slim. What a marvellous creature. The girl
had the same hair except lightened by the sun. Each step
brought a new perspective. The body, shaped by the light,
gentle ease of the limbs, that skin and there were those eyes.
She pushed the door open.

Before her stood a large, slightly dishevelled man. Roughened by the weather with a menacing beard and a black mane of hair. He seemed powerful, as much in spirit as in stature.

"The children mentioned you and said you might drop by but there was no time involved." She had a beautiful sensual mouth.

"Thanks. Hope I haven't arrived at a bad time."

"Oh hell no." She put her hand on his arm, seeming almost amused by his formality.

"Tom and the kids are down at that scrappy bit of sand on the edge of the heath. Bit of a mix of a cliff edge, slope, path ..... Good safe fishing spot. Convinced there's Little Terns nesting there." She paused. "They're rare you know."

"I'm a great admirer of birds but apart from Magpies they all look the same to me and I often get Magpies wrong. One of those projects I have marked for my next lifetime. Learn a bit about birds."

They reached the front of the house. A big old lounge draped with loose covers took the majority of the space. It was surprisingly hot.

"I'm Jennifer. After an hour or so most people tire of calling me Jennifer and I turn into Jenny." The woman held out her hand. Cassems added another note about this family. The mother was very young. She must have born her first child while still a teenager.

"Leo," he said, taking her hand.

"Wow, the great Leo Cassems in our humble house. Tom will be most impressed. I don't think he totally believed Marty when you were casually mentioned at dinner." She looked closer at Cassems. "You're hot. How about some fruit punch stuff.”

Sipping an odd cold mix of pineapple and watermelon, tactfully removing the occasional seed, Cassems wondered if the kid’s mother fed them this same cocktail with a more than a hint of rum in it
He heard the sound of the bird hunters approaching from their search.
They were singing. And the singing was tuneful. Actual harmonies were taking place.
“There is a season, terns, terns, terns ...” They stopped when they entered and found Leo Cassems in the room.
“Tom Brandy,” said the man, moving forward and shaking hands vigorously. He wore only shorts and some leather sandals. He was slim, young, tanned and completed the puzzle on the children’s looks. With a collection of light curls framing his face he had the makings of a Botticelli creature grown to adulthood. He was all golden, even the hair on his chest, though his eyes were more blue than the green of his wife. His voice had a husky quality.
“Please say you’ve heard of the song, Turn, Tern, Turn.”
He spelt the words.
“Yes, I have.”
“See disbelieving rats.” He eyed his children. “People do write songs about birds.”
“Well, it’s actually from ....” He glanced at Tom, caught the conspiracy and said, “Oh.”
Tom smiled at the situation.

Within an hour of his arrival Leo Cassems was reduced, distilled, entangled in the world that constituted the Brandy family. They existed on their own plane and for their own indulgence. It did not seem a conscious act. It appeared they were unaware of any eccentricity on their behalf. The artist was at once charmed by it and wary of some agenda he had not yet fathomed. He could easily be some close relative. They treated him as if their association had begun decades rather than minutes ago.

Liz was a miniature of her mother with slim, effortless movement. Marty was an amalgam of both parents though darker in complexion. Denny the youngest was a smaller version of his father but oddly with a roman nose. All three had the most piercing green eyes. Their intensity took some adjustment. Cassems was convinced they were unaware of their effect on the recipient of one of their glances or stares.

"These," said Tom, laying out a pile of brilliant watercolours on hot-pressed artboard, "are not for my work but for sale. I have a great job but the remuneration is less inspiring. Mainly birds, some marsupials. They add nicely to the budget."

His enthusiasm was all boyish. The paintings were very good. Meticulously detailed and apparently accurate. Possibly the exquisite background vegetation added to their commercial appeal. There was a fair nod to the specimen sketches of the early botanists and anthropologists. A subdued softness to the colours without being pale and unappealing. Cassems quietly admired the patience of somebody who could take their talents and control them to such a degree that they became photographically clear yet still a balanced piece of art.

Over lunch, Cassems decided to ask his question. Denny sat next to him and their arms rubbed as the boy grappled with his food. The whole group in an absolute minimum of clothing that appeared somewhat an afterthought. As he and the boy both reached for the same rough-cut piece of bread they looked into each other's eyes. It was a light moment and after the smiles and gentle jostling, he let Denny take the bread.

It occurred to him and a brief visual search of each of his hosts confirmed it, none of them had but one freckle. Not a mark or blemish. Waxwork purity. Yet they lived, almost totally unclad, in and out of the sun.

Nor were they tanned to a leathery brown. The sort of texture of those who live in a daily baking heat. Instead, they had a pale washed-out look. "Perhaps they have a in-built immunity," he silently mused. Aliens perhaps. A new breed of 'improved' humans. Odd, nothing was quite right and yet from another perspective, it was blissfully perfect.

"I'm being weirdly artistic," he thought.

He caught the older boy Marty looking at him. The boy's smile was so completely unabashed, welcoming and open he could not harbour any more negative thoughts.

He returned to his mission. Though perhaps that had been to survey the situation rather than what came next.

"For a while, I've been poking around a few ideas. Looking for some new directions. Art is like that. You never know where paths lead. Often they fail and you slink back, chastened to try something else."

Cassems noted a silence and that he had their polite interest.

"The first time I saw your children I came upon them by

accident. (He had already mentioned the hole and they had all been amused by the telling of the story.) It was a vision that quite captured my spirit. I'd like to paint them. Build them into the land and their environment."

Damn, blurted it out, he thought. First time we've met. I am an idiot. Surely they will find me very odd and possibly dangerous.

Notebook of Leo Cassems

January 8

'Yeh sure, whenever you like.' (The father - Tom. Shrug of the shoulders.) 'That's fine.' (The mother Jennifer.) 'Oooh, when do you want to start?' (The girl - Liz.)

They seemed slightly disappointed, as if they had been expecting something of greater import to be announced and all I wanted was to paint their kids.

Halfway back on the cliff track I was juggling several concepts. Was the casualness of their reply a polite smokescreen? Are they so damned relaxed with the world that the idea of a total stranger taking their children away to his studio is not a concern? Is the thought of Leo Cassems using any of them in his paintings blinding their judgement? Are they quite astute and still in control and thus am I perturbed at the ease in which my request was granted? The three children will be here in the morning. Neither Tom nor Jennifer seemed interested in coming along. Tom has some Petrels to paint and in fact is then heading up the coast to leave them with a gallery in Narooma. The Jenny woman is going to cook something involving aubergines, possibly mousaka (I love mousaka) and then read a book.

I explained (twice) that I would just be doing sketches. Perhaps some photos. It is how I 'gather ingredients for my paintings' and then 'cook them up' at a later date.

That it goes without saying that there would be no cause for nudity or any disturbing behavior. They seemed quite amused by this last bit. As if it was of no consequence and a rather stuffy statement. If I'd said the opposite I doubt they'd have blinked.

I hope these kids will be controllable and not noisy.

Three children will be hard. How could it be any other way? Our parting was so light. See you tomorrow.

The girl Liz is just twelve, in that brief landfall between childhood and the beginnings of adolescence. How quickly it will be lost. Marty, the oldest boy, is ten. He's more open, less mysterious than his siblings. Denny, the youngest boy is eight. I wonder if he realises as I did that eight is the most perfect year of your life.

CHAPTER 7

A Studio Session

At eight-fifteen, they are there. No running, calling, giggling,
bash on the door arrival. They are suddenly there. They
have entered the house and are in the wooden hall when Leo
looks up from his coffee in the kitchen.
"Come in," he says, unnecessarily, invaded without control.
They peek as they pass by the various rooms off the long
hallway. The bedrooms, the study, rooms full of boxes with
no purpose.
At the end, beside the kitchen as it opens out, all three move
barefoot silently down the two steps into the giant, open
plan living area. Liz slides onto the lounge, giving a tiny sigh.
She lies blissfully with her eyes closed.
The two boys say, "Hi Leo," then join their sister lying
together. The girl has shorts and a tiny top, the boys just
shorts.

Marty opens his eyes. "What do we do?" he asks, his hands behind his head.

"Well, in a way, you have the easy part."

The first session with the Brandy children is a delight. On the big wooden balcony hung over the trees, they slip in and out of his instructions, lock in position, hold themselves naturally, displaying maturity that is breathtaking. Perhaps it is because they quickly forget he is there.

He moves about them sketching, picking at eyes and necks and shoulders. He also takes photos for reference and to save time, concerned that they may revert to normal children at any moment. Become listless, uninterested and unhelpful.

A banter that is an agent for loosening the stiffness of people aware of being observed is hardly necessary but it is kept up out of some loyalty to the system. Very much an extraction process, Leo Cassems learns things about his models. School? Yes, it's okay. Friends? Yes, they know a few kids. Interests, playing and imagining. The future? They're too young to think of such things.

Did their parents make them come to his house? An odd look followed by a quiet, 'no.'

What would they be doing if they weren't here now? Out somewhere thinking, is the answer. But aren't they thinking now? "

'Yes', they say but the thoughts are not the same. Leo enters a new area. So, what are they thinking now?

"That your house is near the ocean but it can't be seen," offers Denny. "From here you can see the approach of intruders on the dirt road but the path at the back is a secret way," adds Marty.

Liz pauses, the eyes are there again. "Your hands are too
slow for your ideas." She gives a half-smile then looks away.

While Cassems absorbs these temporal messages he notices
Marty looking beyond him, gazing about at the house
that looms over him, his neck strained. He looks back at
Cassems.

After their eyes have been locked for some moments the boy
speaks.

"The man who built this house for you loves timber."

"Well, you're right there", Cassems replies, remembering
the Morris fascination with trees and obsession about using
certain types of native wood and grain.

"He got the proportions wrong."

"Pardon?"

"Your house is for giants. You're a mortal size. Room to
grow."

Cassems looks at this kid. This ten-year-old. There is not a
hint of smug, cocky, odious. Just pure insight.

He notes the giant beams, massive high joints and angles.
Art nouveau touches. Morris drove the carpenters to
breaking point with his plans.

"How old are you?" It is a rhetorical question of course.

The boy just smiles the happiest of smiles. Now he is smug,
because he is right.

Deep in the morning, concerned that his models are
approaching critical boredom, Leo offers pies heated in the
oven and cups of tea because he has no soft-drink.

While they sit and eat, he observes. A number of patterns

emerge in their behaviour. They, unconsciously it seems, navigate together whenever they are given the chance.
In this case, they all lay entangled in each other on the lounge. Marty drops a blob of his pie contents onto the back of his brother. With a casual finger, he wipes it off again and licks his finger. The younger boy hardly notices.
Liz picks at a tiny blemish on Marty's shoulder.
The naturalness and casualness of their actions remind the artist of a small group of primates. Then Meerkats come to mind.
He tries to find hints of some deeper more sinister cause. Perhaps sensual. Then shakes his head at following this line and notices the girl watching him. Are they inquisitive, fascinated by everything? Are they slightly rude? Or do all children watch and it's just the intensity of their eyes that makes him notice?

When they are done for the day, Liz insists on him laying out all his sketches on the floor then climbs onto the breakfast bar, her toes curled over the edge as she concentrates, furrowing her brow and squinting.
She directs Marty and Denny to arrange the work in an S curve starting with the charcoal roughs over by the doors to the balcony and finishing below her with the pen and wash.
Leo Cassems climbs up and kneels beside her. Clever little thing, he can see his work coming to life. The images directly in front finally represent the kids alive.
"I like me," she says, leaning on his shoulder, "do you like me?"
"I'm pleased with the progress, Jenny".
"I'm Liz," she whispers sympathetically, "Jennifer is my

mother."
There is a silence. In a more precocious child, it would have
been a way of achieving superiority in their relationship.
With Liz it remained a tiny slip. No consequence.
As they leave Marty asks, "Where's your studio?"
"I can show you if you like but there's nothing much in
there."
The boy looks. "He made a mistake, the man who built this.
He didn't realise that this big lounge and deck are where
you'd want to be and where you'd want to paint."
Cassems put his hand on the boy's head, tilted it back and
looked into his eyes.
"Yes, he didn't realise."
They nodded to each other as though settling some minor
query.

Alone once more Cassems briefly remembered his early days
at art school. The owner of the house in which he boarded
had a daughter roughly the age of the girl Liz. Once a week
he knocked and entered their part of the house to pay his
rent. As if engineered by fate the door was nearly always
opened by the girl. She would usher him to the front parlour
of their very large quarters on the pretext of waiting for
a parent to come and then remain silent. Eventually, the
silence would overwhelm Cassems who would feel the need
to fill the void and utter some mumbling comment on the
weather or ask about school.
The child's monosyllabic replies and looks of triumph and
amusement made him loathe the brat. Assured by the wealth
of her parents to a life of privilege and utter indifference
to her fellow human beings, he could see her useless

existence adding nothing to the world until the day she died.
It inspired his art for a while which became moody with
a great deal of black. He explained the psychology to one
of the teachers on a quiet day. "Ah," said the man. "Best
concentrate on leaving something to the world that will
make up for such people." He liked the man immensely after
that.

Many years later, when he found that this teacher of art
had died, he made a small pilgrimage to a sculpture in the
city. One of his teacher's best works. It surprised him that
he became quite emotional, standing in the rain, his head
bowed.

CHAPTER 8

The House that Morris Built

The architect Morris Yates had done his good friend Leo
a favour. Over fifteen years ago he visited the 50 acres of
bush that his artist mate had just purchased. They put up
a tent and surveyed the odd dish-shaped parcel of land.
It contained a small forest of white gums and paperbarks,
open grass and at the bottom, where the track carried away
up the ocean ridge there lay a sizeable pond with a stand of
she-oaks. It harboured an odd collection of guests from the
avian world. The two men sat under the edge of the sea-cliff
looking into the dish.
"Marvellous location, Leo, marvellous. Incredible that
the Parks Service didn't grab it when it became available.
They've bought up everything else hereabouts."
"The real estate lady is a fan. It was never on the books.
Walked in at the right time. I'm pretty sure she had some

grievance going on with the Parks Service. Didn't ask. It was the fastest conveyancing job I've ever seen." Cassems was quite taken with the simple story of bureaucracy losing out. "Do they bother you? The Parks people," the friend asked. "I never see them. It's a wilderness. There's only two for the whole area. Probably busy with the paperwork. Or growing hemp."

"So, the answer to the high-life is to find a place with no life." Cassems glanced about. "This place is crawling with life. No more women, booze, stupidity, waste but plenty of life."

"For a monk, maybe."

The two men made a cup of tea on a little butane stove. Morris looked at his artist mate.

"You aren't planning to camp here for the rest of your days, are you?"

Leo Cassems shook his head.

"So you invite an architect up for the weekend. Somebody you've known for years. Somebody who will do you a favour."

Cassems sipped his tea staring at the trees he now owned.

"I'll understand if you say no. You're big-time these days Morris. Time is money and I have little of the latter."

Morris cut in. "Two conditions Leo. The building will go there at the top of this dish. It will be tucked in behind the trees and survey your kingdom from above. Nobody will know you're there. The second condition is that you have no say in what happens and you will accept without question and build what I design."

"The second one's a bit tough."

"Leo, you're becoming a bit of a bigshot yourself," said Morris, waving his arms like a messiah, "I know better what you need than you do yourself."

The plans took no time at all. Cassems realised quickly
that Morris was seriously keen to do this project. It was to
incorporate all the pent-up parts of the architect's character
that could not be expressed in knocking out office buildings
and corporate headquarters. The budget blew out but
Morris knew lots of people and called in lots of favours.
The beams and detail in the carpentry became a sore point
with the tradesmen but once the raw construction was
complete Morris brought in his secret weapon.

Charlie Coulson spent many months camped in the massive
house with his basic woodworking tools and his passion
to feed upon. He sat or hung or crawled over the place and
carved out joints that needed no pinning, added curves
and ornamentation that were straight from his head and
the landscape, animals and birds that surrounded him
and polished them all into a living monument to the art of
the wood craftsman. Every part of the building became a
sinuous, flowing wooden environment. The man hummed
tunes as he worked. He was obviously happy. Cassems fed
him. He had simple tastes. Loved salad sandwiches and cups
of tea. Occasionally he would speak.
"Don't know where Morris got his hands on this timber
here. It's beautiful. Really rare, protected. Can't get it. Unless
you're Morris." He would give a little laugh as he ran his
hands over the surface.
"Beautiful."
As Cassems admired the completed works with awe and
fascination he was overcome with dread. He couldn't ask.

It would sound so crass.

There came the day when Charlie stood before him and announced he was satisfied. He had done all he wished to do. He considered his work complete.

"Charlie," said Cassems, "this is bloody beautiful. Beyond anything I'd imagined. Jesus! I don't know what else to say."

Charlie's face lit up. His eyes roved over the work. A mix of melancholy and triumph. He eyed Cassems carefully.

"You really like it? You'd tell me if it wasn't so?"

Cassems who had watched the whole thing materialise could only assure the small man that he was besotted with the place. If it was possible be in love with a physical thing then he was married to this building. He would never leave. Which brought forth the question he had to ask.

"Morris did explain my finances to you I hope. It's going to take a while to pay you for all this."

Charlie Coulson looked at the young artist. "Yeh", he smiled. "Look I gotta get going now. I'm glad you're happy with my work. Would have been a real problem if you weren't," he chuckled.

As he packed his gear into his van he turned to Cassems. "I am a little short. Couldn't let me have a few dollars to get some petrol and buy a meal on the trip home?"

Cassems emptied his pockets of every cent he had and thrust the ninety-two dollars into the man's hands.

Weeks later, as Morris helped him complete the move into his home, Cassems inquired. He'd paid all the bills except Charlie's. When would it be coming?

"Charlie said it's all square. Said you paid him the day it was all finished."

"What?"

Morris explained as best he could. He'd known Charlie for over twenty years. When he first met him through the trade he'd thought the man was quite old even then. He'd done lots of nice work for him. One night over a few beers the man explained he was a wood carver at heart. He'd always been looking for the ultimate project. The one where he would have complete control and no restrictions. When I sat on the hill that day having a cup of tea with you, I thought this is the one for Charlie. Turns out I was right."

Later in the morning Morris retrieved a parcel from his car. He laid a discreet brass plate on the table.

"Here we go," he said, 'this is the one condition from Charlie. He means, instead of sending you a bill. It goes on the wall. Look he's even included the brass screws."

The plate read -

NOTE:

A HOUSE WITH A SOUL.

CONCEIVED BY MORRIS YATES.

CRAFTED BY CHARLIE COULSON.

Feel free to touch.

"That's it?'" said Cassems. "I screw this to the hallway wall and we're even?"

"Apparently the expression on your face the day he finished paid him many times over. Send him one of your first paintings from here," said Morris, "He'd like that."

It took near nine months for Cassems to produce a painting that he felt was the right one for Charlie. It had strong, grand tree trunks and rich foliage, black depth and a sinuous art nouveau undertone in the shape and makeup of the man's timberwork. All the hallmarks of Cassems semi-abstracted view of the world.

He enclosed a heartfelt letter, explaining as best he could how much the house meant to him and how it had become part of both its environment and its occupant. He added that he would be the custodian of this gift for all his days. As a PS he added, 'I like to touch.'

After the package had gone he felt that he may have over-done the sentimentality but he had meant every word.

Several weeks later a letter arrived in a pale grey envelope. It was written by Vivian Coulson. She was incredibly grateful for the painting and was moved by the obvious deep affection that the house had created for Cassems.

Charlie had died about one month ago. It had happened suddenly. She found him on their back patio where he always sat to enjoy a glass of wine and look at their garden in the late afternoon. She liked to think that, as he sat there in that chair, his last thoughts were that he had fulfilled a lifelong dream to produce the perfect hand-finished timber house. Something whose existence had lived only in his mind all those years.

She would hang the beautiful painting in their lounge and admire it every day in memory of her dear husband.

Cassems had sobbed like a child. He sat for a day and late into the night beside his small lake. The water-birds became so used to his hunched figure they pecked around him.

He wished he could talk to somebody. He needed a family

but there was no one. His parents were dead. His older
brother gone in a car accident. He wasn't sure whether he
felt loss, anger or fear. He'd wanted to add Charlie to his
tiny list of people he could trust. A person he could meet
occasionally and know that their conversation would be
honest.
It became a feeling of loneliness.
He snapped back from his reverie when he returned to the
house. As he reached around one of the kitchen's upright
beams his hand felt a small beetle gently coaxed from the
wood by one of Charlie's chisels. It sat there, forever frozen
on the edge of the timber at stomach height.
"I wonder how many more I've yet to find?" Cassems
announced to the empty room. He smiled and everything
was okay between him and Charlie.

A month later he had the idea to invite Vivian Coulson to
the house to see Charlie's work. Once decided he was quite
taken by the idea, imagining himself escorting the lady about
and then supplying lunch on the deck.
When he rang the number a man answered. He was Charlie's
son. His mother, he said, was in a nursing home. She had
suffered a minor stroke and although her health was
satisfactory, she could not travel. He and his wife and their
two children were now living in the house. The children
often sit and look at Cassem's painting. They discover things
in it that he cannot see. He guesses that is a talent we lose as
we grow up. As life takes away the ability to notice things.

The call ends on a positive. He, the son, is also a carpenter.
He has inherited his father's tools. He is going to do his best

to become another wood craftsman.

Cassems likes the idea that he may have sown a seed for another generation to tread upon the difficult road less travelled. He wonders if the reality of tending to a family's needs will interrupt the journey. Like so many great creative works that are never born. Swept away by the necessities and obligations of life until time erodes their chances.

CHAPTER 9

A Visit from Georgie

The bell at the entry rang reluctantly. It carried in its tone and the method of its cow-bell rattle, all the weariness of one who has travelled at great personal discomfort to a place so distant, foreign and obscure as to be akin to visiting the canals of Mars.

"How does she do it?" Leo asked aloud as he made his way to the door.

"Georgie, you blossom. Come in. Yes, I know, frightful trip, terrible people, all out to get you. I've made some tea, virulent blend, hand-picked by maidens and secretly sold in the local shop under a generic brand. Can you imagine?"

Georgie Little, a large-framed, elegant woman, in mid-heeled white sandals and a flowing, lightly flowered cloth creation, followed Leo to the wooden dining/kitchen area. No matter how many times she visited Leo Cassems she was still in awe of the immense house Morris Yates had created. The huge vaulted ceiling, held aloft by massive beams of dark wood. The name of which she always forgot. The endless array of odd little carved creatures added by Charlie Coulson. Then the balcony stretching the area and the eye into the tree canopies. She walked down the stairs leaving Leo up in the kitchen like a nightclub barman and flopped into a chair. "Why Leo, do you keep only hard, rustic, uncomfortable chairs? You look grotesquely well for a change. This is Deborah."

Leo became aware of another woman. Considerably younger than Georgie. Standing in the hallway half-hidden by the gloom. The stained glass of his front door made her a multi-coloured image. She looked remarkably fit. Short cropped blonde hair, a mid-blue singlet and beige drill shorts with cuffs. Leather sandals on her feet. She was tanned and pretty in a muscular sort of way. She carried a canvas bag.

"Hullo, Leo." She held out her hand. "It is really a pleasure to meet you. I do love your work. I'm not just saying that. I heard your life story on the trip down. So, I've officially touched you and absorbed some of your fame. Now I'm going for a swim. Leave you and Georgie to talk. It's down your path and up over the cliffs I imagine."

Leo held her hand.

"Yes, you've imagined it correctly. But please, there's no need. I have numerous teacups. Some with saucers."

After Deborah had bounded off down the path and into the trees, with a borrowed towel and Leo had served tea, he turned to speak.

"Yes, she is mine. A journalist already. She's sweet, highly

intelligent and she hates being called Debbie." Georgie
fluttered her eyes.
Leo closed his mouth. " I hope you're both very happy. And
who's counting." He touched the woman's cheek across the
table. "Hmm, Georgie honey, I've always felt that a woman's
perfume should be something subtle that lingers in the room
after she has departed. A tiny trinket left glittering.
A reminder. Yours precedes you like a raiding party."
"Did you ask me up here to remind me of my nasal
problems?"
"No, but I do need to open the doors to the deck before we
continue. Does Debbie, sorry Deborah, mind?"
"Not that she's mentioned. Perhaps it helps her to find me in
a crowd." Georgie raised a manicured finger. "Before you say
it. No, it won't last. I don't think she's really into the woman-
woman thing. A little unsure and experimenting. So, for a
while ..... "

They sipped tea and smiled at each other across the table.
Mentally they circled. "Years ago you'd be pissed by now
and force gallons of red down my neck till I joined you in
your mess."
"I've mellowed."
Georgie pulled a face. A grimace.
"That's what worries me, Leo. As a friend and an avaricious
agent, I'm concerned .... that you may ... be losing your edge.
Perhaps you should become a drug addict?" The woman
raised an eyebrow.
Briefly, in the silence, Leo looked across the room and
pursed his lips.
"Well, come straight to the point. Attach yourself to the

carotid artery and squeeze."

Georgie looked shocked but Leo smiled. He patted her hand. "Calm yourself, woman. My balls are still mine. I called you up here to look at some new work. I'm onto something. Really pleased. One little moment. Got a fix on a whole range of possibilities." Leo grinned benignly.

Georgie Little said, "Good" and thought 'Thank God.'

CHAPTER 10

And Then They Were Gone

Georgie fumbled her car down the backtracks that had
taken them to Leo Cassems' house. He had produced some
excellent wines from his cellar.
Deborah similarly inebriated to the driver but more aware,
tried to appear casual beside her.
"Don't worry my babe, we'll make it." Georgie patted her
companion's leg then quickly cursed as she negotiated a
tree stump. "I've done this run before. Leo should have this
damned road repaired."
"He only owns the last eighty metres. The Parks Service are
unlikely to care much about fixing the rest."
"Well he should annoy them until they do something.
I certainly would."
"Without a doubt," said Deborah, smiling.

Restored again to a sealed road heading for Tathra, they relaxed. A great bald orange sun lay over the trees fused by heat haze.

Georgie broke the silence and one of her loose client/agent rules and spoke of Leo.

"This new interest Leo has in this Brandy family. I'm more concerned than before when he wasn't producing anything. If they're so damned cutesy and cuddly they should be on greeting cards or if they're really magnificent maybe a photographer should do a session with them but Christ, I can't see Leo getting the results he wants and then he'll be disappointed and go into another bout of pissups and melancholia."

Deborah offered an opinion. "Those drawings and roughs we saw, they were odd. What would I know? But I thought they . . . . can't find the word ...... were very dark, impelling. I like a bit of a mystery. There's nothing better than a rainforest for that. If the paintings go the same way . . . . they were still Leo Cassems. He's pretty distinctive after all. Can't see anybody mistaking the artist."

She squinted waiting to be put in place for venturing an observation on Georgie's turf but the woman agreed.

"You're dead right but art is such a pretentious business, I'm hoping he doesn't try too hard to get it right and start getting all traditional. You know, painting bloody portraits. Next thing we'll have is he'll develop mass appeal. That will be the end of him."

Emboldened, Deborah spoke with a little reassurance, "He's not even slightly traditionalist. That's his claim to fame. He created his own style. Halfway to abstract. Recognisable. Hidden in layers. Well, so far nothing looks like a portrait.

It seemed as if he was blending his subjects together, trying to make them into natural objects."

"Well, whatever he's doing we're going to have to pay a few more visits down here." Georgie snorted and added, "Or have this Brandy family rubbed out."

"He's a really nice guy," Deborah mentioned somewhat out of the blue.

Georgie tried briefly to think of a reply then sighed as if further burdened. "You're not due back for a day. Let's stay at Bateman's Bay tonight. Have dinner in a cafe by the water. Drink something sparkly."

Two wallabies briefly hopped alongside the car. It was all pretty jolly to be on the road to somewhere.

CHAPTER 11

Leo and Jenny

Approaching the Brandy house on the faint heathland track the artist noted that it was quiet. Still, it presented an increased interest for him. Locked in an aspic mould, glistening with a new life that had not dwelt previously in the annually empty building. He paused. It was his nature to observe. More silent than the grass, he knew that at least the children were not inside. Although they could be watching him. He had learnt this much about them already. On the verandah, creaking boards denying any attempt at stealth, he peered once again into the dark interior, the screened door blurring his perception. He knocked.

"Hullo," she said, appearing in the hall from a side room. "I knew somebody was about. The house tells me. Come in," she motioned to him, not bothering to approach the door. "No formalities. Heck, we're neighbours."

Jennifer Brandy, barefoot, walked gently ahead of him toward the generously lit parlour. She wore a filmy, palely printed garment, tied at the waist. Her body was so girlish and amiable, it seemed to play with her clothes. An 'erudite hippy' Cassems mused as they turned to each other in the room?

"You'd like a drink. On a day like this and after a walk, of course, you would." She smiled, that same flittering movement of the corners of her mouth that he had seen in her daughter. "It's the exotic fruit punch stuff you had last time," she said. "I'll put in some extra rum to add a bit of interest."

Cassems stood schoolboy still while his host clinked about in the kitchen. He noted the big heavy table and lounge draped with loose covers. The room had been painted a sandy colour with one wall in dark blue. A number of Tom Brandy's bird and animal drawings hung on the walls. They were all executed with watercolour and pen. The detail was quite exact. The man was obviously very competent. A fine artist. Cassems noted again his ability to combine what appeared to be scientific correctness with settings that brightened the images and made them live. Watercolour had always annoyed Cassems. It was an exacting science that allowed no second chance. He greatly admired those who mastered its techniques.

"Where's the family?" Cassems realised he had asked the question out loud.

Jennifer Brandy was at the door juggling two glasses of punch and a tray with nuts and raisins and dried fruit.

"Oh the little people are off at some secret location and Tom is ……". She hesitated. "He's away again for a few days in the Nadgee Wilderness, photographing wildlife for his reference files. Everybody's off it would seem. Have some punch. There's a lot more so don't sip. It contains rum. The kids love it."

They sat on the steps of the verandah looking out at the two panels of blue representing ocean and sky.
"The children are fabulous. Two sessions. I'm genuinely enjoying their company. Not much experience with kids. I was expecting it to be … difficult. And so far the results are what I wanted. Are they okay with it all?"
"The kids? Certainly. They're having a great time. I think they're curious about how it will all turn out. They'd tell if they'd lost interest."
Cassems smiled. Of course, they would.
Jennifer rested her chin on her hand. "How does an artist know when it's going right?"
"When he knows he's in control. Rather than feeling his way. " Cassems looked at Jennifer. "Was that a trick question?"
She lay a hand on his arm. "No, I've always wondered if there's a point where artists think, this is it, I have what I was looking for, followed by some exaltation."
The artist looked at the hand. "Never underestimate the power of the metacarpals."
A lecturer named Grimby had made that statement in his first year of art studies. It seemed melodramatic at the time but the man's observation held true. Hands where expressive, they spoke and they lied. Eyes, mouth, hands. These were the keys to all humans for Leo Cassems. While the man's main work involved impressionistic

interpretations of the land and nature he kept the Grimby
principle in mind whenever around other humans.

"My moments often come some time after I've finished
something. I notice it again and see it in a different light.
I think, did I do that?"

For an hour they talked in a lazy manner on a range of
relaxed, unrelated subjects. Jennifer lay back on her elbows.
She rarely took her eyes from the horizon. Small patches
of resigned humour hid in her views but Cassems sensed
an overall melancholy. He found the woman intoxicating.
That same easy sensuality that existed in the children
permeated her body and being. He saw her sketched in
charcoal on a pad. The hours of figure drawing in his youth.
He found himself working hard at the conversation as he
tried to remain detached and subtle in the observation of his
companion.

He dearly wanted to ask about her relationship with her
boyish husband but there appeared no opening. It was
somehow indelicate as if once broached it would break a
spell and upset some balance.

"You always seem to be here at the house. Do you ever get
away?"

Jenny looked at Cassems and smiled. "Hell yeah, don't you
worry about me." She lowered her voice and glanced about.
"Since both, the kids and Tom have lost interest in the little
beach down below here, I've moved in. I've even stashed
a chair, some plates and cutlery down in the cave. It's so
peaceful. If you tell anyone I will not hesitate in killing you."
They chuckled together then she added, "I mean it. Like
that." She clicked her fingers.

Once again they fell silent and stared at the horizon. Time ticked on.

"Has anybody pointed out that you stare at people?" Jenny still had her eyes fixed on the horizon while Cassems realised he was in fact fixed on her face."

He told the truth. "All the time," he said.

The languorous mood was abruptly terminated by the appearance between them of Liz. The girl slid onto the step with the same snake-silent tread that she managed in all her movements. As Leo Cassems was startled by the girl's silent arrival her mother was unmoved. Liz put an arm round each of their necks and hugged them to her.

"Hullo my favourite people." She held them off balance for a moment and then let go and placed her hands primly on her knees.

"So we're your favourites," Jenny stated, with no tone to her voice.

"I live for the moment," said Liz.

Marty and Denny arrived and piled on top of their sister, entangling the two adults in their scramble. Leo Cassems was drawn into the melee. Soft skinned children and their beautiful mother. He remembered glancing at her as he held laughing Denny upside down and deciding he could easily be dealing with the legs and arms and laughter of four children, Jennifer simply being the oldest sister.

On the way back from his visit he stopped near the top of the cliff path, easing himself into a seated position close to the edge. Well below to the north, the empty beach lay flat except for a series of spidery footprints running to and fro

with the inevitable hole as their focal point. The Brandy kids
at work again. Where had they been when he walked over to
their house?

In essence, the visit had been a political call to ensure the
parents of his subjects that his work was progressing in a
natural way and that he was not wasting their time. Perhaps
an opportunity to place a thankyou into the conversation.
He was a formal man.

Of course, none of this was achieved. Now that frustrating
family added another level to the depth of their character.
The absent husband, a lonely wife and the enveloping
presence of the children. He wondered how they were
in normal society. This hot beach stage was after all an
isolated, peculiar place. It gave itself to the play currently
running on its salty boards.

In departing, another appointment was made for the
children to sit for him. They happily agreed. No hesitation
or sideways looks. Jennifer was invited. She declined with a
smile. "I don't think art is something that flowers in front of
an audience," she said. "I'll come when they're complete."

Cassems reached down to the large pocket on the leg of his
pants. He wrestled out a fat little artist's sketchbook and a
6B pencil. For unknown hours he drew quite furiously using
a pocket knife to resharpen the pencil. Grass, a gull, a wind
raked tree, rocks, all the flotsam of nature within sight.
He worked quickly in a state of unusual passion. Every page
satisfying, each sketch completing itself comfortably without
a doubt of possible improvement. Then his pencil moved in
a curve. Jenny's jaw and her face appeared on the cartridge

paper. He sketched her face, her hands, her foot. It seemed quite effortless, as if she sat before him.

When he felt the sun biting his arms. He stopped and removed his shirt. He noted a line of difference in the colour of his arms and the less exposed chest. Finally bereft of subject matter and with a stub of pencil left he lay back in the late sun while his eyes closed. He heard wind slipping across the land, felt grass touch his face, all manner of life. Later, in this empty landscape, he made his way along the track and away from the ocean to his home.

CHAPTER 12

Morris Falls

Carefully observed, a trace of sunrise is about. Each
darkened room of the house is revealing its contents in grey
shapes. Above the house, an edge is forming on the trees.
Stars are losing their intensity to the coming light.
Leo Cassems has for some minutes resisted the natural
impulse to turn on a switch, to see his way about more
clearly. He has a plan. It concerns him that it is seriously
immature, yet he reasons its justification in fun.
The Brandy children have been asked to arrive early.
Somehow, in darkness, he feels he has an edge on their
abilities. In desperation, a small reading lamp is used to
enable locating of the last items for this elaborate invention.
As dawn makes its way from tree to tree, spearing a single
heavy summer shot across the ocean onto the land, Cassems
has placed himself in a high position above the track from

the cliff. He wears shorts and sandals and a rough old blue shirt with the sleeves rolled high on his arms. His beard is trimmed back to a point where it is more a healthy stubble. This latter adjustment to his appearance has no connection to these early morning plans but is a manifestation of a new trend in his habits toward neatness.

The track from the cliff skirts the sides of his dish-shaped land as it approaches his house. At the end and to one side, it crosses a wooden bridge to his landing or round to his front door. Another Morris Yates innovation. On one side the tall sub-temperate rainforest timber and ferns cover the slope. On the other side, a grassy run down to the pond. Cassems has placed himself halfway up on the edge of the rainforest. Comfortable, leaning back on a large shoulder bag he now waits for the appearance of the enemy. It can be justified as an academic field exercise. Study of the mode of attack, observation of the subtlety of their approach will impart great benefit on the last drawings before an amalgam of images can begin to form as the final works.
Briefly, he feels foolish but it is this game that has allowed him to appreciate the coming of light to the land once again. A time was not specified in the appointment for this day.
It is instinct alone that has brought him to an ambush position so early. To know a magician's trick, put yourself in their position. How would they perform? With Liz, Marty and Denny, those three children, it is a culture of oddness. Early would mean as day dawned? Or not? Possibly a long wait could be in store.
Humidity hung in the air only dulled by the night. Beneath his body, the earth held onto its warmth. A movement to the

left introduced a small creature from beneath a log.
It had the size of a rat but thicker fur, a shortish furry tail,
high ears. Its movements were histrionic. All that nervous
extravagance needed for survival.
Was it unaware of his presence or merely dismissive of his
threat? Cassems wished he had listened more on boozy
nights in the past when friends learned in the local fauna had
tried to educate him to his surroundings. His resistance, he
justified in not being distracted from his calling.

A jagged line of gold began to step its way through the trees.
Sunlight now spilled over the clifftop further up the track.
The artist, hidden on the hill, surrounded by ferns, let out
a sigh. The bush creature before him vanished with such
speed it could have been the magician's puff of smoke. They
were not going to be early. Still in bed no doubt. Perhaps
he would make breakfast. It occurred only now that he had
prepared lunch but omitted breakfast.

He was not sure why he looked behind. It is that unknown
remnant of our prehistoric past when existence demanded
a constant observation of all that is about. Certainly, there
was no noise. Perhaps one of those enigmatic silences that
come together in nature when all the ingredients of the land
conspire at once to stop. He jumped. His eyes must have
given them victory. They were smiling broadly as they sat
not more than a couple of body lengths away on the slope
above. All three children. Their toes in a neat row on the soft
earth. Shoulders pressed together. An audience to his failure.
"Were you waiting for us?" Liz asked the question. It had no
malice, no victory in its delivery. Just a question. "Or looking

at the sunrise. Its lovely isn't it."
Lying across his bag, staring up at them, Cassems thought,
'I love these kids.'

A small secondary prize of sorts was obtained a little later as
they made their way back up the track toward the cliff top.
At a point beside a giant Swamp Gum, Leo Cassems was able
to step around to the back of the tree and reveal to his three
companions a faint track which plunged back down into the
heavily wooded gullies that lay to the south of his house.
"I am taking you into quite magical uncharted lands," he
extolled.
He noted with a small degree of satisfaction that this new
area was foreign to them. Their eyes gave away a hint of
annoyance that they had not discovered it already.
"We're completely alone now. Nobody about. Best behaviour
or who knows what the consequences may be. I could be
nuts you know."
Liz broke across this childish talk. She placed her hand on
his arm in the same manner as her mother, pushing a palm
frond aside as she spoke.
"You're incredibly sane and nice. There was a bushwalker
camped on the beach so that's somebody 'about' and where
are we going?"
They all stopped and looked at Cassems.
"You're way too pragmatic for your age," he said to them
jointly.
Denny pulled a leach from his sister's arm and flicked it into
the bushes. Then returned his gaze to the artist.
"We're going to a creek. There's a small waterfall and a
swimming hole. I brought towels and lunch. You can swim,

I can sketch. Bit of a reward for your patience over the last
week. Or we could go back to the house."
They all looked at him briefly then moved off down the path.
Cassems took this as high excitement and approval.
The waterhole had acquired the title 'Morris Falls'. He and
his architect Morris Yates had discovered it during the
construction of his house. Cracking open a bottle of wine
they had drunk to their find and in a magnanimous waving of
his arms, Cassems had declared the name in honour of his
friend. A later check of the topographic maps had shown no
name for the watercourse. It remained undisturbed over the
years in this remnant rainforest. Cassems used it by himself.
The possibility of sharing it with various women had been
a tempting option yet none it seemed carried the key that
made him wish to reveal his secret.
He considered this aberration in his logic as he followed
his three small friends deeper into the sub-temperate ferns,
palms and greenery that made up the gully floor.
With little consideration, this small part of his life was given
over in an unexpected way. Yet he felt comfortable about
them knowing. He knew they would appreciate the place
and make use of it. He looked at their backs moving through
the gloom, light and shadow sliding over them. The boys,
as usual, wore just shorts and Liz little more. He could not
recall ever seeing them in shoes and only once in shirts.
Water running could now be heard. The ferns and palms
became moist and the soil spongy. The whole understorey
steamed. Cassems realised he was dripping. He ran a
finger across his brow and flicked the sweat away. With
satisfaction, he observed a line of sweat running down
Marty's back. 'They are human,' he thought.

Morris Falls was a rather grand name for a mid-sized rock
over which a solid tube of clear water ran like an endlessly
filling bath into quite a large deep pool. A collapse of rock
from higher up the gully had neatly blocked the watercourse
at some time distant and from this beginning sand, ferns
and debris from the surrounding area completed the
transformation. Water entered and left the pool at the same
steady rate. A balance was achieved. It was quite deep under
the actual water flow and close to the rocks but had a gentle
slope of sand into the water on the side they approached.
Dumping his large pack Cassems flopped down beside it. He
lay back gazing up through a complex of green. Fine fronds
of water ferns, short cabbage tree palms, higher palms,
vines, trees climbing out toward the light, sections of sky far
above.
Marty's face appeared over him, genuinely excited.
"Coming in?" he asked.
"Maybe later." The face vanished. Shortly after, the first
crash of body meeting water, followed rapidly by two more.
They were in.
It occurred to Cassems that he need not have bothered
with heavy towels. These kids spent most of every day wet.
During the scuffle on the verandah the day before their
clothing still had salty water oozing out onto the decking.
He sat up in order to retrieve his sketch pad from the bag.
He stretched his neck still sore from the bag's weight.
Below him, in the water, the Brandy children were diving
about, quietly exploring their new aquatic habitat. He
watched as first Liz then Marty flipped over and curved
down beneath the surface. As they duck-dived his casual

glance stayed on the spot. What had he seen? He looked to the edge of the pool. Their clothing lay in the grass. They were naked.

This discovery rained a gamut of emotions through Leo Cassems at once. First the artist, whose whole life had involved the close study of the unclad human figure, whose original meeting with these earth children had set in train the concepts that he now developed. He could not help but watch them. They were even more beautiful. With the last trappings of society's conventions flung aside on the grass they quietly frolicked as naturally as wild animals.

No splashing or screaming, more sliding through the water with fish-like assurance. He wondered briefly how the normal prudish disciplines of contemporary existence had somehow been passed over or dismissed by these three.

Then, as harshly as an unexpected punch, those disciplines forced themselves forward. Their apparent innocence, their peace, their happiness would have to be reigned in.

He clapped his hands loudly and called. "Hoy, you lot." It had to be lighthearted. "Get back here and put some clothes on." He added a reason. "You'll get me arrested." It sounded so bourgeois.

Liz stopped and stood siren-like half out of the water, her wet hair hanging down. The first stirring signs of breasts on her chest. They all stood looking up at him, glistening wet.

He could see they had no understanding of his problem.

A silence ensued as they wrestled with the concept.

"What's wrong?" Liz finally asked earnestly. Then she took hold of the situation. Putting a hand on her hip in mock coquettishness, her head to one side. "There's nobody about. You're our friend. You can watch out for us if you

like." She gave one of her totalling disarming smiles.
So innocent and without guile that he was lost.
Cassems opened his mouth, searching for a reply.
Denny added a practical note. "Want to keep our shorts dry."
The obvious retort, "Why now?" went unsaid.
"Coming in now," called Marty, "see who can stay under longest. I'll win of course."
"No," said Cassems, "I'll sketch for now." Still, they understood nothing. Even Liz was acting out a part. If he stripped and joined them he was sure they would not even pause to blink. He waved them on rolling his hand in an odd papal gesture.
They slid back into the water with hardly a ripple.

Cassems sketched for a while then lay back and viewed the high forest canopy with delight. Briefly, he noted that the line of tan on their rumps had been hardly noticeable.
"They are not new to this nudity caper," he thought.
He closed his eyes smiling to be woken in the fullness of time by Denny picking leeches from his legs and exclaiming, "Boy, they really like you."
Marty meanwhile was handing Cassems his backpack with a boy-like 'feed me' look on his face. They even complimented Cassems on his fine sandwich-making. Nothing these kids did constituted normal behavior.

On the return journey, Cassems had the children sit for a while amongst the ferns. The multiple shadows of the leaves on their faces fascinated him. An eye caught in the green-black depths, the side of a face hidden in the boiling gloom of a forest alive with creatures. They were part of

their surroundings. As ever they were patient subjects, not
squirming, simply quiet, observing things and the goings-on
about them.

It was so quiet Cassems could hear the scraping of his Conte
pencil on the pad's heavy paper. He filled in several of the
sketches with oil pastels, afraid he would lose the intensity
of the colour in his subject's environment. He took some
photos but found sketching more satisfying.

When he had a few more pages filled he called a halt.
Marty emerged from the greenery with a gecko sitting on his
wrist.

"I've got a new friend," he said quietly, "it crawled up my
back and down my arm."

"And you just sat there?" enquired Cassems.

"It's best not to make any sudden moves in these situations,"
said the boy with a knowledgeable tone. He held his hand
up to a tree trunk and the lizard, after looking about, almost
reluctantly pattered off onto the bark.

"Of course," said Cassems. The boy's response had all the
hallmarks of Tomdad's training.

Notebook of Leo Cassems

January 10

*Took the kids to Morris Falls today. Really enjoyed showing
them. If ever some humans were meant to swim in that pool
it's the Brandy lot.*

*They had a great time. No screaming and giggling, just slipping
around like delighted fish. Decided to keep their clothes dry for
some reason so jumped in sans clothes.*

*Current community levels of coyness don't apply with the
Brandys. Just so damned natural.*

*I couldn't care. They looked like a part of the landscape.
Decided not to frolic with them. Damn my conservative
upbringing.*

*They jumped out and sat around me eating the sandwiches.
Eventually got 'em to wrap up in some towels. Sort of a
compromise they didn't notice.*

*Came back with my sketch pad loaded to the last page. Quite a
bonus.*

The Diary of Elizabeth Brandy

January 10

Today when we went to see Leo for some more painting.

He was already waiting for us. He took us to his secret swimming hole. It's really nice. Mr Lazy didn't swim, just sat about drawing in his sketch pad.

He calls the pool Morris Falls. It's really nice. Going to go there a lot.

When we said goodbye Leo hinted he wanted to get on with his painting for a while so we'll stay away.

Leo makes really nice sandwiches.

PS Marty met a gecko.

CHAPTER 13

Tom in the Nadgee Wilderness

Near Cape Howe, in the Nadgee Wilderness, there is a small marker that indicates the border between the states of New South Wales and Victoria. It is an insignificant stone block sitting in the sand. A person passing through the area could easily miss the thing or assume it had no great value. It is in fact the top of a very grand and quite tall monument placed on the coastal rocks close to the ocean. For many years it gave a clear statement to those few who came this way that they had reached the border. A local phenomenon that causes coastal dune sand to wander in a strange circular pattern, had eventually buried the marker. Given time the sand that has engulfed it will move on, disappear into the sea and eventually, over many years, re-emerge down the coast and begin to circle round once more.

It was this marker that Tom Brandy had in mind as his turning point, to end his southern excursion into the wild and begin a journey back along the coast north to the ranger

station at the Wonboyn River. Here, he would pick up his car
and make his way home to his family at the cottage.

With a continuing wild national park on the southern side
of the border and a designated and protected wilderness
area on the northern side, this was ideal territory for finding
elusive species to record.

Just before Cape Howe, there is a beach. It is the last beach
in the state. It is a pristine expanse of sand with a line of
higher soil covered in spinifex grass. In the surf there lays
the remains of one of the great number of shipwrecks that
a combination of Cape Howe and the nearby Gabo Island
have sent to their doom. Tom Brandy had no idea of the
name of the ship or the beach but he had camped there
once before and knew that fresh water could be obtained
by digging in a nearby dune. All day he fought through
thick, twisted heathland vegetation. The terrain dipped and
curved dramatically providing a veritable city for birds and
marsupials. He had a camera full of great shots and some not
so great but they were just reference material from which he
could conjure up a complete detailed and correct finished
piece of art.

Late in the day, hot, sunburnt, tired, in close proximity to
his stop for the night, Tom moved along a slightly elevated
sandy track that led through tea tree scrub. The light sandy
ridge, about knee to the surrounding heath provided a loose,
rough path across the low landscape. Suddenly, to his right,
a bright male Scarlet Honeyeater and its less conspicuous
mate hung in the air tantalisingly close. "Myzomela
sanguinolenta," Tom thought. "Oh, this is good." He moved
forward as carefully as the undergrowth would allow.

A short zoom lens on the camera would enable him to bring the birds in but he needed to move nearer in order to fill the frame.

He edged through the thick matrix of twisted tea tree branches not daring to take his eye from the small creatures. They waited. He would get this shot. His day would be complete. Tonight he would celebrate with the contents of a hip flask in his pack. Good whisky. Expensive malt. A treat, a carrot on the end of the journey's stick. Raising the camera, carefully sliding the lens to maximum zoom, turn to focus, the birds snapped into clarity in the viewfinder. One more step would fill the frame. Keeping his eye to the camera Tom Brandy, crouched and stepped. He felt the soft sandy soil give out beneath his boot. He lurched, the birds shot away. Cursing he slid into a small trench in the belly of the land. Already contemplating his bad luck he let himself drop into the soft sand of the hole. It was not deep, he would crawl out and make for the beach.

In surprise, he was aware of something attacking his leg. An initial reaction was that some animal was in the hole. The weight of his pack pushed him down. In a mixture of curiosity and sudden shattering pain, he realised that he could not move. A branch of this cursed heathland timber disappeared into the back of his trouser leg. Already a bright red stain spread out from the breach.

Tom Brandy lay on the nameless beach. Nausea swept over him. In the remaining hours of daylight, he swooned in and out of reality. His hands creaked. Bones ground together. He faintly knew that the dark red on the ground between that cursed trench and his present position indicated a

significant percentage of his blood supply was no longer with
him. Shuddering he lifted onto his elbow to view his leg. The
piece of tea tree still protruded from his bush pants.
The fibrous end that he had sawn through with his penknife
was clotted like a rotting fairground toffee apple with blood
and dirt. It still oozed through the pathetic scarf tied round
for support.
His hands shook alarmingly and he flopped back causing
more pain. Tablets from the first aid kit were having no
effect. Against better judgement, he also drank from the hip
flask. His breathing was rapid.
Above, their wings tipped with gold from the last strands of
western sunlight, gulls swung about calling and responding
before nesting for the night.
Wrapped partly in the blue nylon of his tent fly Tom Brandy
reviewed his situation. Nadgee was a protected wilderness.
He was literally in the middle of a section of nowhere.
Access was restricted, permission needed to be obtained.
Nobody had been this way for weeks. Although he vaguely
mentioned that he would return tomorrow it would not
cause any concern to those that knew him or to the ranger if
several more days passed before his reappearance. Nobody
would start to be worried enough to begin looking for him
for three to four days. Then he had to be found. In what
little examination he could manage Tom Brandy knew that
his injury would kill him very soon. The branch entered his
right leg just above the ankle. Long and thick, the weight
of his body had facilitated its progress into the bone and
from there it had proceeded up behind the calf muscle he
guessed, to nearly as far as the back of his knee.
He squeezed his eyes as a sudden rush of tears ran over his

face. On his back, his breath came in gasps.

Stars slowly emerged in the night sky, the surf swept and cleaned the empty beach and he wondered if the miserable survivors of that wreck in the water had felt so utterly alone.

CHAPTER 14

And The Painter Paints

After some minutes of indecision, flicking through a
large range of CDs, lifting some out then returning them
to the line, it was the sound of the Glenn Miller Orchestra
playing 'Imagination' that accompanied the first series of
brushstrokes of the morning. The music was a memory from
a seemingly distant childhood.

Leo Cassems was unconventional as an artist. He was
organised and methodical, at least at the start of a new
creative push. Music gave a little flavouring to the thought
processes, setting moods, relaying colours. It was the
creamy sound of an old World War orchestra that seemed
right on this bright, hot day. In its structured themes, it
put him in mind of a time when the coast around him lay
undisturbed. Before humans intervened, added it to their
psyche and it no longer belonged to an unknown past.
As the temperature of a new project rose and his passion

ignited, the artist's early neatness lost momentum. The room became barbaric. Eating and sleeping slipped away and he existed on a biblical mix of red wine and perhaps bread if some came to hand. Cassems always worked on a number of canvases at once. He had discovered early in his career that to leave a partially completed work and return to it hours or even days later gave a fresh perspective. He would see the image anew and more often than not be able to enhance its progress with greater insights.

This morning however he lay out his brushes, arranged a table with tubes and jars of acrylic, hung vast bunches of sketches in bulldog clips from a string across the kitchen area, then placed three large stretched canvases on three separate tables. He put a fourth an even larger canvas on a giant easel he had dragged out into the area. He put more smaller canvases on the floor.

'For overflow,' he thought.

His element of schizophrenia buried within would continue as he moved from one work to the other in the manner of a chess champion attacking numerous opponents.

"Circled the wagons, boss," he said, as he surveyed the setup.

Early preparation would enable him perhaps to find an elusive tube or the fine brush he needed at a later, more frenetic period of the operation.

The children were banned, the phone unplugged, in a strange wandering, unrelaxed air, last night he had shaved off the last of his beard. He knew not why but of course, he did.

It left him this morning more eager than he had been in

years to produce something that gave life to the visions that flickered, unresolved through his mind.

By midday, the number of paintings, in some degree of resolution, had increased to six. On one giant central work, the hole on the beach, contained an entwined sand sculpture of the children in early stages. Another caught a fleeting representation of their presence within the depths of the forest. A third, the most recent canvas propped on a chair for viewing, contained the outlines of the face of Liz as she stood glistening in the pool some days before. The pool owning her as an extension of its natural force.
Cassems had not sketched this scene but as he worked the image appeared in his memory urgently making itself available. He took another prepared canvas and without hesitation laid the face and those eyes on the surface.
She would be part of the water. Like light on the surface.
An annoying flicker, hard to see, difficult to comprehend.
The artist smiled at these connections. Someday he might tell her of his inspiration.

He paused in his work staring into the summer sky beyond the windows. He could see none of his subjects as adults.
It was a trick he normally found easy. The boy in the old man, the mother in the small girl, dignity in the moment on a young man's face before he returned to the mask he wore for his peers. Yet the progress of the Brandy children, past their present state, eluded him. He bowed his head in concentration. No, nothing came to mind except stereotypical images that were not of his making.
He knew the answer. It lay buried in the longing within all

people. The wish to retain a moment, to stop time and hold onto something that is perceived as ideal.

Those kids, this hour and these days were part of an endless tide that carried its cargo away.

Next summer, they may all be back. But, they will have been replaced by strangers and he will look into their eyes and know that what they briefly had was now gone. Similar perhaps but never the same.

An irretrievable part of the whole.

The paintings that now took up his time, adding like some manic calculator to the sum of his frustrations and little triumphs would be all that was left. Even a change in the weather could break the mood, stealing away what he fought to achieve. He quietly thanked Morris Yates again for the huge, vaulted area with its equally large outer deck. Room to move. To concentrate.

By evening Leo Cassems was elated. As the afternoon progressed he found himself growing in confidence. Upon each work, a mix of lines, light and colour outlined a piece that he wanted to achieve. His pace quickened with the dulling light. He grew impatient. His hands needed wiping with torn newspaper as paint began to go astray. He searched for brushes that then had to be cleaned in order to place a new shadow or subtlety. It was time to stop. He should step back but the rare accomplishment pushed him onward should the moment desert him.

A black patch in the grass below the balcony bore testament to the fickle nature of his creativity. Days of previous work, in other years, hurled from the railing and burnt in a bonfire of frustration.

Now he had a room in which he was surrounded by fresh
material that he loved.

Just past 10 pm, he allowed himself some fresh wine.
Dragging out a cask of mysterious burgundy he sat in the
room's centre, his head turning from one painting to another,
determined to extract a fault. It was his way. No critic could
match his own steady line of questioning.
These paintings were all at Stage One of his process.
They contained the skeleton of what he wanted to achieve.
He liked to work this way.
As little Liz had pointed out, his mind raced ahead of his
hands. The remedy was to lay down maps, a line of pebbles,
so that when he returned to the canvas to add in detail,
solid colours, blacks and shadow and fill in parts, to bring
the whole thing to a point of completion, he had enough
information already there to point the way to what he had
envisaged. This was achieved by quickly laying down a wash
of just one or two colours that captured the idea enough to
give life to the vision.

He could not see one of the tightly propped canvases that
failed his eye. A warming glow of satisfaction welled up
inside. The delightful feeling of exhaustion and satisfaction
at the end of one of those rare days when all is right in
one's endeavours and nothing more can be distilled from
a moment. Sleep would give the neurons time to recharge
and reorganise. Tomorrow it would all come together, a new
batch would begin and the task of filling in detail, colour,
texture and the touches that would start to give each work a

life, they would all begin.

These early stages were fraught with uncertainty. At times the finished product lost its freshness and vitality in the progress from the initial outline to the finished, completed work.

He had confessed to his art teacher once that he was afraid to touch an initial sketch because it was so perfect he felt any further work would ruin the whole thing.

Instead of ridicule, the man agreed.

"We all suffer from that," he said. "You wouldn't be an artist if you didn't appreciate such dilemmas. As you advance in your training you'll learn how to be brave enough to press on."

Cassems became aware of a noise. Initially, he thought of possums coming out for their periodic exploration of his roof. Then the door rattled, a half attempt at knocking but the door opened and something came padding along the hallway boards, down the three steps through to his encircled canvases. Between two paintings, in the darkness, Cassems saw a face. It was Marty. He was crying.

The boy saw Cassems as he rose from his chair.

"Marty? What's up, mate?"

The boy squeezed between the paintings smearing yellow and black paint on his chest and green on his back.

He lunged at Cassems and cried again. This time in a complete break down of sobbing. No explanation came forth. The man sank back into his chair cradling the boy's head. He put his arms around him, slightly surprised at how light and small the child had become. The boy shuddered in his torment.

They held each other for some moments then Cassems took the boy's head in his large hands and turned Marty's face to his own. The boy's eyes were vague, as if trying to comprehend an enormous problem.

"Marty," he separated the words, "What is wrong?"

CHAPTER 15

Emergency

In the darkness of his big four-wheel drive, Cassems concentrated on the road. The wine, his need for sleep and his empty stomach meant that he should not be driving. He felt the circumstances warranted a degree of recklessness. Jenny sat beside him her hands clasped on her lap.

In the back, the children huddled together. In an odd presence of mind, he had wiped the paint off Marty and got them all to wear shirts. Shoes were too difficult but it was a slight adjustment to civilisation.

"I told Marty not to go," Jenny repeated, shaking her head. "I told him not to bother you. He just took off. Nothing would stop him."

Cassems growled at the woman. "Have you any idea how pissed off I would have been if you hadn't asked for my immediate help?"

Tom Brandy lay in Bateman's Bay Hospital. The message said
that he was desperately ill. A ranger hunting a rogue dingo
found him on a beach attracted by the flapping noise of
some tent sheet. The probability of this happening was, from
the broken information they received, incredibly unlikely.
The father and husband of his passengers was unconscious
and his life in danger. The ranger had satellite phone.
He'd called in a rescue chopper. With paramedics.
A police car finally found Jennifer at the cottage after
her being traced through Tomdad's mobile phone and
neighbours at their home. It had relayed all the information
they had available then left on another urgent errand. They
were trapped. It was then that Marty decided he could not
sit and wait for developments.

"Are you all related?" The nurse looked about the group, her
eyebrows raised.
"These are my children," Jennifer replied absently.
Cassems smiled back at the clinical face of the nurse. "I'm a
friend. I did the driving. I'll wait outside."
"Oh, there's no need. He won't know you're here I'm afraid."
The nurse motioned them forward down the corridor.
"I thought you liked to limit the numbers for intensive care,"
Cassems commented.
"Oh, Mr Brandy isn't in intensive care. Just sleeping off his
operation."
They entered a room near the end of the corridor. One small
lamp shone and Cassems noticed the street lights through
the window before he noted the presence of one bed in the

centre of the room.

Tom Brandy lay enshrouded in white and connected to various monitors. A drip ran to his arm and his right leg was elevated in a sling and appeared to have a drain running from beneath the padding and crepe bandages.

The children made for the bed gathered at both sides and took their father's hands. They said nothing, all staring intently at the man's face.

All the boy-man handsomeness had escaped. The figure on the bed looked gaunt. His mouth hung slightly open, his lips dry. The effervescent glow that marked his good health had drained away replaced by an emptiness of pale hues.

Jennifer stayed at Cassems' side. He heard her say, "Oh God, Tom, what have you done?" She simply lowered her head and then held onto his arm.

A young man appeared in the doorway. Aside from his white coat and stethoscope, he bore all the earnest characteristics of a medical person. Cassems would have assessed him as a doctor anywhere.

"I'm Dr Cooper. No doubt you're anxious for some news." He raised his eyebrows in the same way that the nurse had done.

They stayed at the side of Tom Brandy for hours while he lay in his drug-induced silence. Jennifer and the children could do little but watch him breathe and touch the supine body occasionally for reassurance.

Cassems observed them from the shadows of a chair near the window. Even now they were fascinating and beautiful. Tom Brandy was a lucky man. A phrase that appeared frequently in the doctor's summary. Even though they were a small hospital, they'd decided to operate here rather than move him again. A top man from Canberra had done the job. He was nearby on his holidays. With no relatives available, consent was waived.

Leg damaged but saved. Strong concern about infection. Blood transfusions, antibiotic drip. Sedated, lot of pain. Very lucky man. Wound must be drained. Long hospital stay.

Dr Cooper had taken him aside after all his reassurances and asked quietly how close Cassems was to the family.

Without hesitation, he had replied, "Very close."

"Well, there's something I think you should know. We're using an anti-biotic drip."

He paused.

"If everything does not go alright, well there is a possibility that the wound may become septic and the leg unsavable."

Cassems looked at the man's face.

"And then?"

"Well, we'd have to amputate immediately." The doctor seemed anxious to go, as if he'd said too much. Then he looked at Cassems again. "Major blood loss you see. Even with a transfusion, he's very weak. He may die."

"Then shouldn't he be in intensive care?"

"It's not like that. Monitoring won't help. He needs more .... luck."

Dr Cooper looked at Cassems.

"I believe in being honest. He's a very fit guy and he should come through this okay. It's just the range of possibilities is wide. I felt I should tell somebody."

Cassems said, "Thanks, I appreciate the information."

Dr cooper turned to leave then put his hand to his mouth. "It's curious," he said, "one factor in the patient's favour is his choice of the wood to penetrate his leg."

Cassems looked curious.

"The wood."

"Teatree. The oil has antiseptic, antibiotic properties. I think it helped a lot."

Finally, late in the night already moving to morning, they left the hospital.

Cassems found an all-night truckie's stop. Nobody wanted to eat but even the children accepted takeaway coffee with some extra milk.

Retracing their earlier route in the hot air along a totally deserted road, Cassems thought of the correct words to use. Each phrase that came to mind sounded contrived.

The children lay in a huddled, sleeping bundle in the back seat. Jennifer sat silently in the front her hands clasped on her lap once more.

Spontaneously Cassems put his great, paint-smeared hand on hers and said, "I'm not a busy man. I'm available at any time. Driving, shopping, leaks in the roof, I'm your man till we get Mr Tom back on deck."

Jennifer gripped his hand. "Thank you," she said and gave a little sniff.

He realised the surge of creativeness that had manifested itself through the day had now completely removed to some holding pattern. Like the story of Taylor-Coleridge and 'Kubla Khan', he would have to take up the challenge again after this interruption and hope that the thread could be relocated.

Internally he gave his own resigned sigh.

When they reached the house there was a noise in the distance. A light to the north and the faint sound of talking. The light flickered. It was a campfire.
They carried the children in and placed them all on the big verandah bed. Jennifer managed Denny while Cassems took Marty.
"Can you get Liz?" Jennifer said straightening the bed.
Returning to the truck Cassems wondered briefly if he was meant to wake her and lead her to the house. Finally, he reached in and lifted the girl easily in his arms. She gave a start and looked vaguely into his eyes then she hugged him tightly as he carried her in. Jennifer smiled quite benignly as he appeared with his cargo.
Once their task was complete Jenny looked anxiously through the window at the distant light.
"Probably just a bunch of happy hikers." She sounded unconvinced.
"I'll stay." Cassems plumped a pillow on the big lounge.
"This looks bloody comfortable and I'm too stuffed to go home."
He held Jenny's arm briefly.
"Go to bed, Tom will be fine. Your world has not ended. We've all just been given a reminder about appreciating life."
He lay down after she had bid goodnight, pleased with the words.

The Diary of Elizabeth Brandy
January ?
*Leo carried me in and put me down gently. Now I'm awake.
Tomdad, you said, "No good praying to something that isn't
there." What if you're wrong. It's worth a try.
Please, whoever you are, if you're there, somewhere, don't
take him away. He's half of all we've got. We need him a lot
more than you do. I don't know how much I love him but it's
too strong for you to resist. He wouldn't be any good without us
and we wouldn't survive without him. I want him back please,
please please, please , please please, please, please please,
please , please please and a million more.*

CHAPTER 16

In The Morning

When morning came it filled the room with a dim gold.
Cassems who usually rose early, lay unmoving allowing his
eyes to search the ceiling and his ears to seek out sounds of
existence. He hoped he hadn't snored. The house creaked as
it warmed, a gull called some way off, there may have been a
hint of ocean in the ambient background hiss.
Cassems allowed himself to slide back into the comfortable
unconscious world he had left.
He must have slept again. There is a smell of coffee. A most
lovely sight. Jennifer Brandy holding the mug close to his
face is sitting beside him on the edge of the lounge. He lifts
up onto his elbow and takes the cup.
"Funny how caffeine can penetrate sleep."
She is both sad and reflective in the action of handing him
the drink. Her gaze is loose and moves about the room.

"God, that's good. A drug and a thirst quencher." He looks at her seated, watching him.

"Did you get much sleep?" he asks. (I slept well. Perhaps I snored.)

"A little."

"How are the kids?"

"Not sure, They've gone already. Off somewhere. It is summer after all."

There is a silence. It extends, blank as a drawn blind.

"Kids are resilient," he says.

"I don't think they understand. I hope they don't. When they have a problem they go off somewhere to sit and think. At least that's what they've told me in the past."

"From the time I've spent with your three children, thinking is something they definitely indulge in. Possibly too much. Still, it makes them rather wonderful."

Jennifer is unresponsive. She is pensive, her head to the floor. He realises her shoulders are shaking. He jumps up. Holding her, seated on the lounge, uttering phrases of comfort, the like of which he imagines are expected in such situations. Her head rests on his shoulder.

They stay together for some time in the silent house, as the sun creaks the boards. She is quiet now. Her face lifts away. Her eyes are closed. She leans her mouth against his in the gentlest way, still salty from her tears.

It is a dreamlike, their act, almost silent, cathartic, ritual rather than passion. Something that needed to be done. A puzzle to be solved. A curiosity that they both should tick from some list.

He is amazed at the beauty of this young woman, the mother
of three, who is so sensual and alive. He finds himself an
observer as well as a participant. Noting her breasts like
those of a teenager, the line of her thigh is committed to
memory, her neck, the sparkle of fine hair on her shoulders.
They move together stretching out the urge to be as one.
Once it is over there will be the need to face each other
again and make conversation and pretend things.
When their actions do conclude it is, like the physical
contact, in silence. They lay together she draped over his
body, her eyes closed, resting, holding the part of her life
that should not occur again.
What have they done? Already he feels as if he has broken
some fragile perfect structure.
"Will he die?" she asks.
"I don't know."
"You can't imagine how much I love him."

In this strange world he has entered, Cassems can now
makes sense of their actions and her statement.
This woman and the husband they have just betrayed are
like brother and sister. There is a greater bond. He is merely
a sub-plot in their lives.

CHAPTER 17

A Return To The Studio

At the top of the cliff path, Cassems finally lifted his head
allowing the surrounds of his territory to encroach. He had
decided to walk back. He wanted some air in his lungs.
His vehicle would be at their house ready for the next visit to
the husband and father.
Time changed. It sorted through situations and moved parts
of the whole. Twenty-four hours and the approach to his
house, his work, the collected experiences of recent weeks
were shaded, now monotones. In the sandy base of the
track, scattered footprints. Small bare feet. He had not seen
the children. Perhaps they were old marks.

At the house, he waited for their appearance. Leaping about?
No, subdued considering current circumstances.
The building lay deserted. Adrift from its normal scope of

sound and feelings.

In the studio area, the children did appear, crept about the corner of the eye, held themselves breathless and still in the images of the boards. They were unfinished, beautiful in their incomplete selves. He stood for some time. Who had done these perfect things? It pleased him that he did not recognise his own work and could admire it as a traveller visiting upon his creative cell.

Cassems next reaction was fear. Would he be able to find the line again? Without this track, he could do little but grope about patching what had already taken place.

He had produced so much in a short time. The next session needed planning. He doubted his ability to rediscover these elements too many times. Elusive creative strands someone had called them in the past. In youth it is easy but the act of ageing brings doubt and the need for reasons.

There was the lounge where Marty had cried out the news of his father's injury. On the carpet, a near-empty glass of wine sat exactly as he had placed it down in order to make sense of the crying child before him.

On the wooden deck, with some bitter remains of a bottle, he sat for an hour enjoying the silent tree canopy. Tuning in and out to distant noises.

A wattlebird worked its way up a tree branch then slipped off into the woods. A magpie suddenly dropped down to the balcony rail and looked frankly annoyed at finding somebody in its territory.

For some moments the artist and the bird shared the uneasy space. They stared fixedly at each other, until an agreement was forged with the raising of an eyebrow and the shifting about of some feathers, the bird moved on and left the man to his thoughts. His thoughts were many.

Notebook of Leo Cassems

January - Can't think of the date .....

Tom Brandy has almost died and I have been intimate with his wife while he lies in hospital.

Schadenfreude?

No, that's cruel.

Somehow it does not matter. I like them, this family, too much to be the cause of their collapse. While she initiated the proceedings I was a willing participant. It all seems irrelevant. A momentary thing.

I wait in vain for guilt, however, my notes here will be the only record of events. Should they be read upon my death then so be it, I will not be involved in any consequences.

God, how casual. Never put anything on record that you would not want seen.

To be the complete creative master in a human world you need a degree of callous self-regard that is beyond me.

Would some being greater than me, have ignored the child, called the family a taxi and continued with his complete focus on the process of painting these pieces?

Was I weaker or stronger in my actions?

Even asking these questions shows a degree of narcissism.

God, man! Just get on with it and drop the analysis.

CHAPTER 18

Tom Returns

Twelve days after his accident Tom Brandy returned to their house by the beach. Disregarding the advice of the eager Dr Cooper he discharged himself and promised to remain on his back with his leg elevated, follow a strict regimen and take a range of medications without fail.
And attend medical appointments, rehabilitation and physiotherapy.
The man was obviously still discomfited as they drove back from the hospital. For Cassems it was the end of an arduous time of painting, in between ministering to the various needs of the man's family both in transport and endless reassurance as to the future prospects of their father and husband. He had purchased groceries, even cooked.

They had collected the car from the ranger station with the

blood-covered gear in the back. Although Jenny now had transport he continued to drive them back and forth to the hospital.

Perhaps he need not have become so involved but these four people had a way of including him so completely that he began to suffer a degree of metamorphosis into an extra member of their group. Their naturalness still surprised him. He would wake on the couch at times when he stayed, to find one or more of the children asleep alongside or find them and their mother wandering about naked in search of some item of clothing. It was not Bohemia revisited, it was them.

Tom Brandy would have a limp Cassems decided. But then the man, who was possibly not supposed to be alive, continued to surprise.

He lay about, painted as best he could with his leg in the air and looked less well and decidedly lighter of frame. No talk of them returning to their home. Perhaps the cottage was the best convalescent place. The children did more hovering about than was normal. They kept returning to their father to touch him and hug him as if checking that he was still there and still okay.

Dr Cooper had chatted to Cassems about a theory he had developed to explain Tom's recovery, failing to notice that he had espoused the theory to him previously.

"Tea tree," he said, "the oil has antiseptic, antibacterial properties. I think it may have lessened the chance of infection. He's so fit. I'd keep telling him how serious his situation could become. He'd just shrug and say,

"I have too much to do to be dead, yet."

Cassems made light of it.

"Well he has a point. It would have been damned inconvenient."

"Inconvenient?"

"Being dead."

"Oh, yes." The doctor smiled. "I'd never thought of the cessation of life as inconvenient. But you're right. I suppose it is."

Cassems hovered about a little, had earnest discussions with Tom concerning art and its place in society and slowly extricated himself from the drugged existence that the Brandy family exerted upon him.

He saw a chance now to slip out of their lives for a while. Time with these children and their mother had given him some insights that only close contact could reveal. The minutiae of existence that glues a more general scene together. Instead of finding a crudeness beneath he had encountered an even deeper vein of gentleness.

At times the prettiness of their lifestyle, the way they interacted, the casual hint of sensuality in their contact with one another and with himself gave reason to question it all. But the most careful observation could find no hint of pretense.

"I have it," he announced one evening after dinner, before Tom's return. The hospital visit had already taken place in the afternoon and now in languorous heat of the evening, the children crawled over him on their giant lounge. It was just what they did. Their skin was dry to the touch. Odd again. Jennifer moved off to the kitchen.

"You people are alien," Cassems continued. "No, perhaps the

last remnants of a fairy kingdom. Look, that's it, I can make out the remnants of wings." Cassems ran his finger over Marty's shoulder blades.

Denny was intrigued enough to ask if his wing stumps were also visible. His brother drew him away. They sat on a chair facing Cassems.

"We're definitely not fairies," said Marty.

"Elves then." Cassems tried to rescue the boy's masculinity.

Liz had not moved. "What about me?" she asked, kneeling up, moving close to Cassems' face in a slightly precocious way she adopted.

"You, could be a high priestess, but I can't see your wings because you keep them hidden. Very clever."

The girl warmed to the idea while the boys scowled. This was a very old fashioned conversation.

"Who would be your favourite?" Her eyes, green and pure did not blink or shift from the man beside her.

Cassems decided to stare back. "Oh naturally, the high priestess, Queen of all the Underworld would be the one I most admire." They continued to stare. A smile crept out from the corner of the girl's mouth. A triumphant smile.

"Elves are really bad dudes," Cassems concluded.

The Diary of Elizabeth Brandy

January holidays

The world is okay, I think.

My Tomdad is back and we are one again. Leo fusses over him more than Mum. He tries not to be nice but he is.

And Mum watches. Strange Mum.   .... Love Mum.

Five is good. Don't know about six. Are we one too many?

Leo says I'm like the Queen of the Underworld. I'll show him that costume one day. Midsummer Night's play. It's midsummer. Good time.

Love is a weird thing. I don't understand it. It can be too strong and uncontrollable and scary.

Maybe I'm only a little girl, with a lot of growing up to do.

Mrs Colby said that last year. Schoolteachers think they know everything.

CHAPTER 19

Escape To The Studio

It was this extra insight that had Cassems now wishing the Brandy family a brief farewell and hurrying back to his own home.

He locked the door for the first time in a number of years. Closed all blinds, shutting away at least the feeling of welcome. He tore off his respectable clothing and put on loose shorts, together with a large shirt. The shirt was a favourite from the past. It had spots and daubs of various paints from previous studio sessions. It had become a sort of uniform akin to the old blood-spattered aprons of nineteenth-century surgeons. A self-imposed piece of psychology. He was back in business.

Handfuls of paint-hardened brushes were discarded. He broke out new hog's hair and sable brushes and dumped

them into a jar for selection. Paint, water, acrylic medium, rags. A large collection of tins, jars and boards for mixing. A substantial new range of fresh tubes and pots of paint. Slightly surprised at how many boxes of paint and other art supplies he had available, till it occurred to him that Georgie had probably been carting the stuff up here on previous visits. A sort of insurance policy for when and if he started painting again. He could hear her, "Wouldn't want the bastard running out of umber, black or blue and abandoning everything in the middle of an urge."
He chuckled.
He had the afternoon and the night.
All the wine was depleted but a substantial amount of whisky would suffice. As an afterthought, despite his urgent need to start the painting process, he prepared a large casserole in a slow cooker. "At least I won't starve," he said to the assembled canvases.
"Oh God, I hope I can pick up the thread again."

Time passed. Days, followed by many more days. Light and dark had little influence. When exhausted he would flop onto a couch and sleep only to wake and notice something on one of the works that needed his attention. Sometimes he would pause in his determined urge to put his mind's eye on canvas. With a sip of whisky he would look about and be pleased but always his fingers moved as he anticipated the next step to take.
What had Liz said? 'Your hands are too slow for your ideas.' Damn the child and her astute observations.

Leo Cassems smiled. He looked from one painting to

another, many now finished, some near-complete, others in outlines of wash with the finished work still implanted in his mind. He peered at the charcoal sketches, he touched the paint and the eye, part of the face of Denny hidden in ferns, staring at the viewer.

He consulted photographic images on his laptop computer to remind himself of some tiny aspect of some scene that his mind had filed away in the 'important' section. Colour, body, eyes, expressions, mood and more. When he stepped back he was pleased.

"Drunken sot produces something worthy," he said. And another week passed, then more.

Notebook of Leo Cassems

Late January

I must write this before I pass out. Interesting medical fact.

The body, even mine, needs rest.

Working 24-hour shifts eventually catches you out.

I now possess the little Brandys. Will sound deeply disturbed and maniacal to a reader of this scrawl in the future but I have every inch of them on canvas. They are mine.

I've frozen and pureed them, mashed, moulded and preserved them in artistic metaphorical jars. Now they can never escape. What a delightful world they've taken me to. If I try to explain,

*to thank them, they'll give me that special look. So I'll thank
them here on paper. You may understand someday, Denny,
Marty and Liz.
I only caught glimpses of the place you inhabit mind you but
enough to steal. And when you've gone and the landscapes you
trod are without you once more, I will have them locked away.
Should laugh in a dangerous fashion about here.
Can't focus on this bloody page. Oh sleep where is thy ....*

CHAPTER 20

A Rescue

Georgie Little used her key.

"Here he is," she said, picking her way along from the dark corridor. The great artist was emaciated, dehydrated and triumphantly asleep in the midst of a jungle of his creation. "Who's been a busy boy then?"

He did not stir. A faint trace of motherhood ignited within Georgie. She became quiet and let the prostrate man's repose continue. About her were artworks of varied sizes. Mostly finished, others in process but recogniseable. They covered most of the far wall. They blocked light from all windows on the south of the building. A deep perspective of some forest pool. Rich with green and black, light cutting in at places. His creatures, his children, slid about in the pool. Shadows of life captured in a bowl.

Other smaller works gave depth to the theme. Faces frozen

in foliage. A tree blended almost with a human form standing alongside. All dark and rich with black and green and hints of light.

Moving past the artist, past the fortress walls of his surrounding images she approached the two giant paintings. Below them, unseen until now, was another huge work.

It showed sand. A deep indentation in the sand held the Brandy children. She stood and viewed it for quite a long time, unmoving, drinking in the effect. It was, to the woman's cynical eye, the most striking, powerful image she had seen for many years. Georgie Little permitted a tear to run down her cheek. It was a secret luxury she allowed herself on rare occasions when emotion was able to surface. All too briefly it would pass. This was a business after all and following a number of years of concern, Leo Cassems was about to reemerge. Something she had perhaps abandoned as a possibility after his last love affair dashed itself on the rocks of indulgence. But by God, he was back and Georgie allowed herself to think in secret joy that she was the first to see some masterworks.

"Oh, lovely little Brandy people," she said very quietly.

"I once was blind but now I see."

In the kitchen Georgie, hard-nosed and practical, searched about for the ingredients of a nutritious meal. The task was not easy. Supplies of anything of note were low, gone or unfit for consumption. Eventually, triumphantly, a meal emerged. Odd in parts with pasta and frozen bits of vegetables and meat but sufficient to sustain interest and thus life in her charge.

She repeated throughout the process that she was

performing an act of selfish, business-based, charity in order to guard an asset. Still, she enjoyed waving the coffee under the nose of Leo Cassems and watching his response.

His eyes fluttered. "Jenny," he said, followed by, "Oh, good God, Georgie, what? ....", then staring about and blinking. He ate the meal with all the enthusiasm of a starving man. Georgie watched, contented.

"Jenny?" she thought.

CHAPTER 21

Lyle Has Some Photos

Very much in keeping with its ink-stained, hurly-burly
origins, the third floor of the 'Herald' building still had
an open plan and a tense atmosphere that plucked at the
nerves of newcomers. Carpet hid the harsh old boards
and softened the noise. Faintly humming workstations had
replaced typewriters. Copy boys no longer existed in the age
of the downloads and transfers. The old gents who swept
up the swarf on the comp room floors were all retired into
history.

Across this expanse of veterans and hustlers there lay a
broad spectrum of knowledge, experience and tactical
guile. Lyle Bennett viewed the heads and happenings from
his smallish desk in the corner by the lifts. Their rumbling
disgorging, engorging presence annoyed him but allowed the
advantage of knowing who came and went or was currently

present at any given time.

Freshly returned from holidays he awaited a call from one of half a dozen 'seniors' who would find some distasteful part of their assignment that they wished to offload. Chasing up a loose end, a secondary interview, researching the tedious part of a feature to pad it with facts. It was varied at least.

Lyle had a need to gain entry to the glass-walled office on the far distant side to his own.

It contained the imminently unapproachable Max Ghent, revered Editor in Chief. A man who worked very much on the tiered system of management. Lyle Bennett had something he considered 'of interest'. It sat just below his line of vision in his shoulder bag under the desk.

He leaned back, looking down past the broken zip to a yellow package in the interior. Nobody had called him all day. Perhaps not used to having him available again after a break.

Ghent was the only man who should see his prize. Political death to try a direct approach, yet who to trust in this room full of egos. To have any of them take the package to the editor would mean that he, the sole agent in their creation, would be reduced to a minor role while his representative obtained most of the accolades and the by-line.

Outside, the day that had begun as a collection of bright blue squares through the windows now clicked to dark as a southerly change drove up the coast. It turned the city to a twilight wilderness. Lyle's despair grew darker with the clouds. 'Old news is not news', Ghent was known to say. Immediacy is all.

Through the dim desks, weaving in athletic confidence, came
one in whom Lyle could place a gut-feeling, modicum of
trust. Always a little special he thought. God, she's so pretty.
A feature writer who did and said what came to mind. Too
good to bother with the survival skills that others employed.
A runner of the race and the only competitor.

On his feet moving in a contour of interception without
intent. Not to put the quarry or the observers on alert.
A casual meeting.
"Say, I'd value your opinion on something I picked up on my
holidays (no, no, say vacation here, sounds smarter).
Could you spare me a moment?" Should work. Need to get to
a neutral corner. An empty room.
She stops briefly. Time to be in position. Now moving
forward. Perfect, open space, out of hearing range.
"Lyle," she says, "I didn't know you were back."
(Lyle gives his little speech).
"Okay, I'll swap. An opinion for you then you chase up some
facts for me at the Mitchell library."
What a superior smile.

CHAPTER 22

Easter

Leo Cassems is on a mission. It occurs to him that this mission is rather annoying.

He is heading along the familiar path to the Brandy family beach house. Months have passed. Easter has arrived and summer has lost some of its edge. Still, he is hot. Only the nights are a little cooler.

After Georgie's visit to raise him with food and reassurance his life has been a Georgie Little inspired whirlwind.

"Woman can smell a profit like an Orca lining up a seal," the man mused.

Unfinished or lesser works had been finished. Whether he was happy with them was inconsequential. Some were off being framed or mounted. Others, for the sake of some idea of rawness, richness, spontaneity, closeness to the artist and his creation, all Georgie's words, were left just as canvas on their stretchers.

Somewhere, some time back, Cassems had caught Georgie in one of her numerous visits and said, "God, Georgie, I haven't seen the ...."
"Oh, they've long gone," she announced with a loose handed gesture of dismissal. Her eyes were on his sketchbooks and the possibility of framing some of the pages.
"What?"
"I swear Leo, you live in another dimension, dear. Holidays don't last forever. They came over to say goodbye. Couldn't raise you. Weeks ago."
"How do you know all this?"
Georgie thumbed through the sketchbook giving little triumphant noises as she encountered some of the more detailed pen work.
"Saw 'em on the road as they were on the way out. Now, this is really nice Leo. You've got to let me frame all of these."
Cassems was not interested.
"And you've just thought to mention it now. Jesus, Georgie!"
The woman stopped. A desperately bright lipstick smile spread across her face.
"I'm sorry, darls." She touched his arm. "I know you think the world of them. But you did only just remember yourself. They said see you at Easter. Not too long to wait. Now back to these sketches. Come on, concentrate."

"Bloody woman." Cassems spoke aloud to the bushes and beach as he skirted past.
She had organised a major exhibition. The publicity machine was already whirring. It was all she could think about.

He was also angry with all the guilt he carried. Angry that he was angry about it in the first place. He had not even asked for their phone number and had only a vague notion of where they lived in the city.

Now it was late afternoon and he made the trip he had made each day for the last four. Just in case they came early.

"Careless, thoughtless, self-absorbed bastard," he remonstrated. "Befriended them, used them, intimate with the wife, husband ill, left them to it, didn't say goodbye. What is to become of you Leo?"

Cassems was in fact atypical of his breed. Forgetful but basically kind. He secretly knew of this fault and was pleased that despite it being an alleged prerequisite for the successful artistic life, that one must be a miserable and selfish type of human, he had succeeded in his profession.

The house stood empty. Gold in the lowering sun. He was sure today would be the one.

School was over for the break. But no, maybe tomorrow. He was quite disappointed. He sat for a moment looking down from the sandy ridge where the track opened out to the grassed area around the building. A forlorn sight. One of their towels lay on the ground below the verandah. It must have been hung over the rail to dry then forgotten. The wind had lifted it from the rails and left it crumpled on the grass. Cassems made his way down to the house. He retrieved the towel and walked up onto the verandah, folding it as he went. He could smell them in the material. Odd, sweet animal smell. Not sunscreen or scent?

Cassems gave a derisive snort. "How can they even smell nice? Really."

He stood holding the towel thinking of whether to fold it and where to lay it down.

A sound? Faint, far off. Then suddenly much louder. A vehicle engine, coming along the track. Coming here.
Cassems felt like a schoolboy caught with a dirty magazine. How embarrassing to be found moping round their house.
He considered making a run for the track but the greater embarrassment of being spotted mid-flight stayed his urge to get away.
In the brief seconds he had before the machine burst into the opening he made the grand decision to use the situation to advantage.
Now the vehicle rumbled to a halt on the other side of the house. A moment of silence then doors slammed. A whoop of pure joy. Denny.
"Get back here. Unload first." Tom.
He heard them enter the house. Items were dumped indoors. Windows opened.
"Damn, I've missed this place. Never thought I'd say that." Jennifer. She continued. "Come on, hoppy, don't overdo it." Still a limp it seemed.
Cassems had placed himself in a nonchalant pose on the large wooden verandah seat. He gazed over the heathland to the sea as he listened to the family reclaim their house and bring it back to life.
"Fridge on?" "Well, get that stuff in there before it melts."

He was now pleased that he had this situation. Soon they would burst out onto the verandah. At first they would not notice him then there would be a moment of madness and a lot of laughter. He might have giggled if he had thought of it. A pair of hands slid across his vision and clamped over his eyes. "Guess who?" A breathy, whispery voice asked next to his ear.

After a brief shock. He hoped he hadn't jumped. Cassems thought, "How the hell did she open a squeaky screen door and get across a large expanse of warped floorboards to my back? And how the hell did she know I was here anyway?"

"Hullo Liz," he said.

The girl hugged him from behind and kissed him on the cheek. Denny, Marty and Liz then launched themselves over the seat and enveloped him.

"Came over to see if you'd turned up and I heard your car," Cassems explained. He noted the boys were wearing t-shirts. "Second time in history," he thought.

"Did you miss us?" Marty asked eagerly.

"Yeh, I guess I did a little."

'Well, we missed you a lot," the boy replied. Once again Cassems realised he'd been outflanked by the honesty and openness of a child.

"Perhaps more than a little," Cassems said, trying to make up some moral ground.

Both boys untangled themselves from their guest.

Denny called through the screen door. "Guess who's here?" As one, the two boys leaned their hips against the balcony rail and stretched in some strange animal joy of being alive and being here. They then both slipped off their t-shirts and flicked them back onto the seat. Turning to the sea once more they lifted their arms, put their heads back and soaked up the sun like thirsty men with a quenching drink.

Denny glanced sideways at Cassems. The artist imagined the

child thinking a line from his own childhood book readings.
Something like, "Isn't this grand."

Dinner took place on the lawn. The sun stayed long enough
to light their meal. At first, there was some eagerness to
move a table and chairs from the house. In the end, they
laid out rugs. Tom was propped up with a box and cushions,
keeping his injured leg out straight. Cassems tried to emulate
the flexibility of the rest of the group by sitting cross-legged
but in the end, gave up and lay on his side then on his back
and soon became a pillow for the children.
He apologised many times for not saying goodbye. Finally
Jennifer leaned over, put her finger across his mouth and
said, "Leo, we get it. Here we are again. It's all good."

Liz looked up at Cassems. "Want to know why we're not lying
on Tomdad?"
"Okay, why?" said Cassems.
She whispered in that movie soft/harsh voice.
"We bumped his leg," the girl half smiled, "we're banned."
"That was weeks ago," Tom said, "hurt like .... hurt a lot
though."
"Doesn't do his exercises enough," said Jenny, glancing at
her husband. "Going to end up with a permanent limp and
become unattractive. People will point at him and throw
stones."
"You just wait and see," replied Tom.
Cassems stayed out of this one. Obviously a sore point.
"We wouldn't," added Denny, after a moment of silence.
"Wouldn't what, mate?"
"Throw stones at you."

Tom held out his arms. "Come here, my favourite child."
Denny got a hug while Liz and Marty feigned disdain.

Wine bottles emptied. Jennifer had the children inside
preparing some coffee.
Jennifer lay beside Tom with Cassems opposite.
"They make very good coffee," she said to Cassems
enquiring look. He could hear the coffee grinder being
wound in turn by the democratic three.
Tom sighed. "It's official ...." The silence went on.
Then he spoke again.
"It is so very good to be alive."
More silence.
Cassems finally asked. He felt he should.
"I've never been in a position even vaguely like yours. Sitting
at the doorway to departure. Looking at the big old iron
knocker and wondering if I should give it a rap. What's it
like?"
Tom stared straight ahead.
Finally he said, "Thanks for asking. Jenny wouldn't."
Jennifer now sat up and rested her chin on her knees.
She fixed her eyes on the sea.
"I'm not sure whether I'm better off or worse. Being
reminded of your mortality in such a way that it stays with
you every day. Life isn't as much fun anymore. I'm sad. We all
know we're going to die. It's a part of the human condition.
It's something that's going to happen. One day. With friends
and family gathered round and hopefully some profound
comment on existence to leave as you go."
He paused and looked at Cassems.
"What scared me most is that I was alone. There is the

knowledge that death is something you have to do alone but I just wanted somebody to talk with, to be sitting beside me. I cried for that, not for death."

Cassems met the man's gaze.

"Your sadness is contagious," he said. He glanced at Jennifer. She stubbornly stared straight ahead with lips tight, her eyes full.

Cassems asked, "No Gods to pray to?"

He was almost relieved by the answer.

"Religion is just a human invention. Helpful for controlling ignorant masses I guess but no use to me near death in a hopeless position."

Cassems smiled in the dusk. He had harboured a notion that maybe the Brandy family were a secret bunch of religious sooks and this would explain their apparent wholesomeness. Now he had contrary evidence he loved them even more.

"I screamed out the names of things I loved, one after the other. I screamed and cried and I screamed and cried until I lost consciousness. Jenny, Liz, Marty, Denny. Over and over. I thought they were the last words I was ever going to say."

The three people sat together looking out at the last trickle of light on the ocean. Jennifer took her husband's hand. She turned to Tom then looked at Cassems.

"Thanks for that little session. I couldn't ask. Tom and I don't have a lot of close friends. Like you."

Her face shifted and her expression changed. Cassems looked round.

The children were standing behind them. Liz held a tray with cups, spoons, biscuits and a pot of coffee.

"How long have you been standing there?" Jennifer asked

quietly."

The children's faces were crushed. All three had tears running down their cheeks.

"Did you really call our names, Dad?" Liz enquired.

"Like you wanted us there with you?" Marty asked.

Tom twisted round and looked up.

"Put the tray down Liz," he said quietly.

He held up his arms. "Please. Come here."

There ensued a great deal of hugging as if the children never wanted to let go of their father again. Then they wanted to hug all three adults together.

After some considerable time in the darkness, Cassems took a chance.

"You know," he said, "you're a very insecure family."

It worked. They laughed a sort of relieved laugh and sniffed guiltily.

After a while Liz stood up, brushing her shorts. Ever the thoughtful one.

"I'll go and reheat the coffee."

She paused with the tray and looked back over her shoulder.

"Now that you've confirmed God doesn't exist, you know we'll have to invent one."

Cassems watched her triumphant departure.

"Precocious child," said Jenny.

"Out of the mouths of children," he thought, "probably how it began in the first place."

CHAPTER 23

The Gift

It did not end there.

Two days later in a frenzy of anticipation, cuisine and
household chores, Cassems stood in his kitchen stirring a
big copper pot with the hint of red wine emanating from the
beefy mix inside. He decided to leave the bay leaves in a
little longer.

Like most artists he was a good cook and believed most
things could be improved with a dash of booze. He had
baguettes, cheese, fruit, wine, mineral water, fruit juice,
entrees.

In his mind, he continually scrolled through the list
searching for the glaring fault that would bring this evening
undone. He had driven great distances to assemble all the
items he needed.

The giant house was clean and above all, tidy for the first

time in years. It smelt of furniture polish. He realised this in turn smelt a little desperate but you can't put it back in the bottle. On a positive note, the time he had put into running a cloth over all the accessible wood had brought him once more into contact with the intimate creations of Charlie Coulson. He had paused at one stage and said, "See, Charlie, I'm touching." He smiled as he recalled it was also something he noted the Brandy kids often did. Quietly, almost reverentially running their fingers over a possum's face or a hidden native mouse. They said nothing nor seemed aware of him watching. They were just at one with the little timber creations.

This was a special occasion and he wanted to impress.

He was not sure why. Perhaps in contrast.

The Brandy family were coming to dinner.

It had occurred to him when he made his way home from the emotional roller coaster two days prior, that he had indulged in and accepted the Brandy's hospitality many times but never returned any. It was a wrong that he needed to immediately correct. Too late that night but at first light the following morning, Cassems trekked back over the cliff path to his neighbors. He was right in one aspect of the visit. Though the sun was still fingering across the land, these people were already well into their day. Grandly he had invited them to his place one day hence for a "bang-up meal and other merriment."

They had accepted his invitation, his apologies about the lack of earlier invites and smiled at his fluster. For once he had not stayed. Hurrying back, his thoughts were scrambled, "Bloody cliffs. Getting fit at least. Bit of muscle tone breaking

out," he muttered. "Bang-up meal and other merriment? A bit grand and silly, Leo. What merriment? House is a mess."
A little further on he stopped and ran his fingers through his hair. He spoke to a bird resting in gnarled tree.
"Menu, hell what do I cook? Paintings, hell do I show them the rest?"

The occasion presented itself for another reason. The artist needed an excuse to give these people a present. He was terrified they may not like what he had to offer.

Cassems glanced at the clock. Something he rarely did in his particular life. He was somewhat surprised that he possessed a timepiece and that it still functioned. Modern battery technology or Georgina he pondered? There had been a vague mention of arrival an time. This adding to the pressure that he may well have already been invaded by those ghostly children and their silent feet. He stirred and prepared and made nervous furtive checks on his surroundings, convinced he would find one the Brandys frozen behind him, about to pounce.
With the giant table laid out, wine ready, food ready, bread and fruit in artistic repose as a centrepiece, the man paused.
"It's all done. Who's a clever lad," he announced to the room.
The reflection lasted a little past a moment.
There was a subdued but firm knock on the front door.
It startled Cassems. Nobody knocked. Certainly not the Brandy kids.
He approached the door ready to see off any intrusion upon his evening plans.

There they stood. All five of them. Glowing in the light of the evening and Cassems' floodlights. It was Tom who had knocked.

"We drove," he said, "thought we'd arrive neat and tidy."

"Um, fine, well come in, come in."

Cassems followed the group down his corridor. Tom still limping along but seemingly more at ease.

"God this place is big," Jenny exclaimed, running her hand over the heavy woodwork. Sliding her fingers round Charlie Coulson's dreams.

"Dark, curvy, heavy timbers. Art Noveau? Beautiful," she said quietly. "You even have some stained glass. It all works. It's how it should be."

Bringing up the rear Cassems looked at the children. Marty and Denny wore white shirts tucked into their shorts. Liz had on a lacy frock, also white with little touches of electric blue woven into the cloth. They, all three, wore brown leather sandals.

Jenny noticed him staring. Their eyes met.

"Shirts ... a frock .... footwear," he murmured.

"Mum made us dress up," Liz explained "and she wouldn't let us sneak up on you."

Tom cut in loudly.

"Damn right. 'Bout time you kids learnt respect for a man's sanctity and that of his castle. You all get away with far too much of this tomfoolery."

His mock rage ended. The second the last word had passed his lips Tomdad knew that he had lost the moment.

From a slightly concerned look, all three children bubbled up and burst into laughter.

"Tomfoolery? What were you thinking." Jenny patted her

husband's arm.

First Denny then Marty sidled up next to Cassems. They both turned their heads in a surreal smile and looked up at their host.

Briefly, Cassems didn't get it then realised what the others could see.

He also wore a white shirt, khaki shorts and sandals.

"It's a smart look," he explained, "surprised it took you so long to copy my style."

Marty nudged him and Denny winked.

"Eight years old going on fifty," Cassems thought as he patted the smallest Brandy on the head.

They toured the house and the near surrounds until it was too dark to see.

Back at the table it was a slow happy time. Food was consumed at a pleasant pace, the conversation was intelligent and varied. They all loved Cassems' Cassoulet. The boys white shirts displayed tiny portions that had missed their mouths. All three children were allowed a small amount of wine with their meal. This had the effect quietening them down considerably. They each sat with a vague, crooked smile and gazed about loosely.

In the middle of an interesting chat about sand dunes Liz looked Cassems in the eye and said, "Where are the paintings? They're in that room you didn't open aren't they?"

"That's a bit rude," Jenny remonstrated her child.

Cassems felt his face flush. He had dumbly hoped the question would not arise.

Jenny looked at Cassems. "We were assuming we'd see them," she suggested.

Best to own up.

"I've decided not to show you. Yet! Because, obviously I want you all to come to the exhibition. I want them to be displayed properly. To see them as the finished work. Most of all I want you to realise how much you mean to me and how much you three children have helped put me back on whatever track I'd fallen off. Can't be done with a quick flick through the stacked canvases. Has to be just right."

He paused, then almost pleading said, "Tell me you understand?"

Silence - then, there it was again. So nice but so annoying.

"Yes, of course, sure, great idea. We'd love to be there .... etcetera."

Why were these people so nice, so damned understanding? Why did he always feel cheated when they didn't show a sign of at least annoyance.

"Actually, I only realised how I'd like you to see them when some went off to be framed and I knew they weren't coming back. Did you ever think you wouldn't be at the exhibition? I mean I'd have sent some local thugs around to kidnap you all and whisk you to the city in a van, if that was what it would take."

Tom laughed. A healthy laugh.

"Hell, miss an exhibition by our friend Leo Cassems? One that might contain bits of our children buried in works on show. Not likely."

It was time for the gift.

They waited while Cassems disappeared into some dark corner of the back of the house.

He returned, hidden, except for his legs, behind a large

rectangle, that was covered with a muslin cloth.

Seating the whole family in a row on his lounge he closed the big doors to the deck. Insects were flying in, attracted by the light. Now, with the lights up he stood opposite.

"I've been working on this for a while. The day I first saw the altered beach from the clifftop its been floating around in my mind. Wouldn't mean much to anybody else. I hope it means something to you all. Please accept this as a reminder of this summer."

He withdrew the cloth.

The Brandy family all leaned forward. They squinted a little. Like a row of lights coming on along a waterfront pier they all began a knowing, universal smirk.

To Cassems' relief it appeared enthusiastic.

They rose one by one and moved closer, bending to see. Small snorts of recognition came from their lips.

Cassems could not move, being the prop that held the painting. He watched their faces as they found the detail of his work.

What they saw was a long stretch of coastline. An aerial perspective. Incredibly detailed.

In the foreground, darkly plotted, was the building they now occupied. It appeared to be almost down inside the bottom of the picture.

Further on the cliff dropped away down again to the beach. In the centre of the beach, there was a large hole. Inside the hole lay three figures, curled in repose. Beyond the beach, over the dunes and heathland on a smaller headland stood a weatherboard house. On the verandah a woman stood. She seemed to belong to the building. Near the edge of the coastal heath a man stared at the sky.

It was not the great man's 'style'. It had taken many hours
over many days. He kept being drawn to the work, adding
pieces. Items from memory that must be preserved,
included, to achieve the objective of a visual diary.
He used fine sable brushes and worked with his glasses
perched on his nose until he was satisfied with the result.
He knew other noses would be pressed up to these images to
savour their meaning and memories.

For some time the painting was examined from all possibles
angles. Cassems continued to prop the work up while heads
moved about before him, taking it all in.
Finally the Brandy group stepped back and looked him in the
eye.
Jenny shrugged. "It's okay, I guess."
Liz exploded across her mother, giving her a solid elbow to
the ribs. "It's fantastic! Mum you're horrible."
There were other jokes but the tide of feeling toward the
painting was overwhelmingly positive. They loved it.
Perhaps because somebody had given them a permanent
piece of their life. Something to display, watch and
remember. Its value would increase as the years changed
things. It would remain what it was while they moved on.
A brief argument took place when Liz suggested she would
be having the painting in her room. This was quickly but
democratically voted down.
Still Cassems stood holding the painting, smiling as he
watched the interplay before him.
Finally Jenny walked around the painting to the artist. She
hugged him and kissed his cheek. "It's undoubtedly the best
present we've ever had and will almost certainly remain so."

She hugged him again and kissed his cheek once more. Liz watched them strangely.

They left at 1am. Cassems carried the sleeping Denny. Marty and Liz supported each other along the corridor, both in need of sleep and under suspicion for having indulged in some more wine while others were preoccupied.
"I think I've discovered that alcohol helps my limp," said Tom at the door. He was carrying the discarded sandals of all three of his children.
"I've found it has endless medicinal properties," offered Cassems.
Jenny and Cassems carried the painting to the car, wrapped again in its muslin cloth.
It was then discovered that it would not fit in the car. After further discussion, the masterpiece was tied to the roof rack and Tom was threatened with a most horrible curse should it be damaged in any way.
"Are you okay to drive, Tom? You can always stay here."
"I'm fine. No highway patrols through here. Can't speed on these tracks. What can I do, bump a tree?"
Handshakes, hugs, kisses and a promise to be in the city in two weeks at the gallery.

CHAPTER 24

Morris

Perhaps a sign of his wealth, perhaps a desire to arrive
unannounced. The Mercedes slid like some gondola on a
calm Venetian lake, to a stop in the hushed, early morning
bush clearing that served as Leo Cassems' parking area.
There was his muddied 4WD, not locked, full of the detritus
of the man's life.

The driver of the large car alighted. He wore a cheesecloth
shirt, jeans and hand-stitched boots. On the wrist of his
tanned arm hung a Rolex which he consulted as he walked
toward the house. It seemed quiet. He smiled at the silence.
He pushed his keys into his back pocket, ran his hand
through his hair, at the same time remembering that he had
picked up the habit from Leo Cassems. He proceeded over
the small wooden bridge to the door of the artist's house.
There he hesitated. Perhaps it was a bit early. His body

rhythms were somewhat awry due to his very recent
arrival from the other side of the world. He had stopped
on the way down the coast and slept for an hour after a
wave of weariness swept in unexpectedly. Despite his busy
international lifestyle he still found flitting between time
zones hard to handle.

For some minutes he stood back leaning against the timber
rails at the front door. He still loved this place. In all his
years in the business this was still the only project he'd
ever undertaken in which he was given complete freedom to
travel down whatever design path he chose.

There were some that came close. Yet, always, at some
point in the process, the givers of such freedoms invariably
starting poking around in the entrails and in the most hand
wringing ways began making "little suggestions." From that
point, emboldened by their first "minor point" the whole
thing would run away with itself.

The visitor remained, in a state of remembering, of times
when both he and Leo Cassems were lesser mortals. It is a
state of the human condition that the past, in simpler times,
can offer more than all the fulfillment of later goals.

What a joy the construction provided. Cassems had liked
everything he saw. He said nothing as per their pact but it
was apparent in his demeanor. Leaning back, from under
the porch it was possible to see the tower he had added, in
the belief that artist's need to be able to climb above their
surroundings. It was a bit of his own junk philosophy.

A perspective thing. He wondered if Cassems ever made the
ascent.

Looking along the lines of timber on the outer walls, he ran his eye down to the sandstone foundations. Great lumps of rock trucked in to form the massive base for the timber bearers. The outer walls showed no signs of sagging, no interruption to the run of perfect horizontal planks.

Could it be that Cassems had indeed heeded his dire warnings of the potential for termite infestation.

Then, he remembered and smiled, tilting his head back in almost a laugh.

Carboni Pest Services! Knowing his friend's lack of diligence in matters not directly related to anything that was of immediate interest he made a deal with a big Italian chap. The closest he could find.

"Once a year, drive to Mr Cassems' house and do whatever you have to do to keep anything getting into the woodwork and foundations. I don't want the area turned into a toxic chemical dump, just keep them at bay."

"Sure, I can do that. No worries," the man had replied, patting his truck full of equipment.

"I warn you, Mr Cassems is an artist. He may be disagreeable. If he gives you any trouble tell him it is on my authority."

"I been chased by snakes, dogs and an old lady with a shotgun. An artist don't worry me."

On that reference Mr Carboni was hired.

He would question Leo about the arrangement's current state of play.

It was while he was crouching down to check the condition of the timber deck that a voice said, "Oh, for Christ's sake, who are you and what do you want?"

Framed in the doorway, wearing shorts, a grubby shirt and a

foul expression stood Leo Cassems. His hair was tangled, he
was unshaven and his eyes were struggling with the light.
A brief silence ensued.
"A cup of coffee, perhaps some breakfast and an update on
Mr Carboni."
Cassems peered at the crouching figure. He grunted. Made
his way to the visitor.
"I got a feeling somebody was lurking about. You know
how it is, something isn't right. Thought it might be a
lost bushwalker or some bloody fan. Knew it wasn't the
Brandys. They'd have just barged in. Turns out it's a famous
architect."
The two men embraced.
"When did you get into town?" Cassems slapped Morris
Yates' back as he ushered him into the hallway.
"First plane in this morning. Who or what are 'The Brandys?"

In a fair mood and delighted to have time with his rarely
seen friend, Leo Cassems cooked toast, eggs, bacon,
mushrooms, some exotic sausages he was keeping for
himself and served it all with home-made chilli relish from
the town. He brewed coffee and the two men sat on the high
balcony to observe their surroundings and each other.
"Bought an expensive espresso machine a while back. Does
a nice job but I usually need three cups. Too much trouble
to go through all the drama for each cup. So back to the big
pot of filtered stuff. It's damned good to see you anyway."
Cassems raised his coffee mug.
"So how long are you in the country?" Cassems asked.
"Two weeks. Maybe three. Can I stay here?"
"Hell yes. Be great, like old times. What about Alice?"

"She stayed in Paris. No, our marriage is fine. I've got to plan up some restoration work for the National Trust and she didn't want to pull the kids out of school."

"All the same man, leaving your wife in a city full of Frenchmen. Very courageous. And how are your kids, anyway?"

Morris looked at his friend. "They're growing up to be little frogs. They speak French more than English. I've got to get them back to Australia. They're so pale they're almost see-through."

Morris Yates leaned back. He put his hands behind his head and took a deep breath.

"Damn, that was good, this is good. Can't beat the smell of eucalypts. Now before I forget. Was checking the old place over when you interrupted. Does Mr Carboni still come and give the place a periodic blast of chemicals? If not, why not?"

Cassems looked across the table, lowering his head and glowering at his guest.

"That bastard. Oh yes, he's a regular all right. You might have mentioned he liked fine food and red wine as much as I do. He comes every three months at least. Brings more food than his fee is worth. He ruins my day and my night. I finish up bloated and nursing a huge headache. We sing ridiculous songs from his childhood. He cries a lot and laughs till he chokes. He gets seriously pissed if his soccer team isn't winning. The last visit I woke up on the floor here to find him asleep in my bed. I hate the man. He has a good eye for art though."

"So, you're the best of mates and he likes your paintings."
 Cassems paused, "Yeh, that pretty much sums it up."

"Does he actually spray the place while he's here?"

"Sometimes, yep I think. No, I'm sure I've seen him do it."

"Amazing'" said Morris. "Now, what are Brandys?"

"That, my friend," said Cassems, "is a considerably longer story. I'll fetch a bottle."

The men on the balcony stayed through two bottles and more coffee. They viewed the remaining paintings and sketches that Cassems had at hand, as he filled in more detail about the odd family that had inspired his new burst of energy.

Morris Yates was enthusiastic about the new work but then he had been a major fan of Cassems style since the day they'd met.

After lunch they walked up to the clifftop and gazed down on the beach where the famous worm hole had first appeared to Cassems. It wasn't there today.

"Sounds almost biblical," said Morris, his hair wafting in the stiff breeze, "someday there'll be a religion based around the sighting of the first great wormhole. You'll be the prophet and these kids will be some sort of messengers from whatever God you like to glue onto the story."

The idea took hold and seated on the grassy cliff edge they embellished the religion with ceremonial procedure, prayers, cloaks and funny hats as well as some innate ground rules concerning eating, drinking and being merry.

Finally, Cassems lay back and said, "We sound like a couple of Uni students trying to outdo each other with how witty and intellectual we are."

Morris looked down at his friend. "Doesn't hurt to be silly occasionally. Having kids has taught me that. I'd have thought your association with these Brandy kids would have

loosened you up. You can't tell me they
haven't pulled that broom out of your arse a few times."
Cassems didn't answer. Of course the man was right.

The relationship of these two old friends was such that
they could exist seamlessly in close proximity without
interrupting each other's need to get on with their own
business.
That day and the next, Morris Yates occupied the dining
table with his computer, phone and notebooks. He seemed
to spend more time reassuring people in the National Trust
regarding the work than actually doing the work.
"Such is your lot when dealing with these types," he
explained, "you're about to do major surgery on one of their
babies and they're as clucky as any mother hen."
Cassems grunted a sort of acknowledgment. Having Morris
in the house caused him, by some untraceable logic, to
re-examine a number of his paintings and drag them out for
some adjustments or fine-tuning.
At one stage he worked on an image of the three children on
the beach with their backs to the viewer. They seemed part
of the sand. Only Denny had his head half turned, as if he
had become aware of the viewer behind.
Morris stood and admired the work.
"That's powerful ….. and just a little bit …… spooky."
"Spooky?" queried Cassems. "How eloquent."
"Well," said the architect, moving to take in a different angle.
"There's something slightly threatening."
"What, about the kids?"
"Yeh, I noticed it yesterday when you were showing me.
You've given them a touch of otherworldly malice. Are they

nasty little people or is it all in the mind of the artist?"

"Bloody hell," said Cassems, "all in the mind of the architect.
Nicest damned kids you could meet. I've built them into the
landscape as part of the environment they inhabit.

No malice. No slit your throat in your sleep. Damned voodoo
psychologist. You've spent way too much time in Europe, my
boy. How many boozy nights have you been indoors away
from the cold with a bunch of Oxford/Cambridge/Sorbonne
types, analysing the crap out of things that have no need of
analysis?"

Morris looked at his friend then burst out laughing.

"You handle criticism much better than in the past. You must
be mellowing."

Now Cassems began to laugh.

"So, how many nights?"

Morris looked.

"You mean the analysis thing. Yep, you got it. Nice people
but way too intense. Given enough time and wine, they could
find the meaning of life in my table leg.

What a time they'd have with your paintings. I guarantee by
the end of an evening they would discover that you were
jealous of the relationship your dog had with the neighbour's
cat."

Morris paused.

"Am I going to meet this wonderful
family?"

Cassems came straight back.

"At the exhibition which I hope you might attend. Not here.
I'm having a break from them to get everything finished."

By mid-afternoon Morris Yates was yawning. He hunted

Cassems out in one of the back rooms.

"C'mon, let's go and crack some waves. Like the old days."

Cassems looked less interested.

"It's been a while."

"What? You lived in the surf when you first got here. What's happened?"

"I don't know. I just stopped bothering."

"Lazy bastard. Well, it's like riding a bike. You'll remember."

As they arrived at the edge of the white water Cassems said, "I'd come down here some days, walk in up to my waist, stand for a while, let out a huge sigh then just head back to the house."

"Wow," said Morris, "if I'd known you'd progressed to long sighs, I'd have rushed back sooner."

Both men dived as a sizeable wave confronted them as it rumbled into shore. The sudden rush of cool water had them shooting out the back of the wave to be faced by another. They duck dived again as it ploughed over their heads. They surfaced further out. The waves had lulled.

"They must have been numbers six and seven," Morris said.

"Woke me up though. Does that seventh wave thing still work?"

"I'm sure it does," said Cassems. "If not I've spent a lot of my life counting waves for nothing."

They chatted for a while treading water, occasionally sliding under the forming waves.

After a particularly large wave belted into shore Morris suggested a count.

"That had to be number seven. So the next will begin the count."

A reasonable wave slid past. "One," they both said.

At four, in a calm between the waves, treading water, their minds drifting in the peace of the day, Morris Yates suddenly jolted and let out a scream. High pitched and piercing it echoed about. Cassems saw a look of terror on his friend's face as he seemed to rise out of the water then flop back. Thrashing about and beating the ocean he stared down into the depths, constantly moving, trying, it appeared, to walk to the shore.

"Something had a go at my leg. Something went for my leg. Jesus, not even sure if it's there."

Now the panic was spreading to Cassems.

"What? The thing or your leg?"

Both men twisted and turned searching the surface for signs of a predator.

About now Marty Brandy's face eased into view behind Morris. His head just appeared. He slid his hair back and wiped his eyes, spitting out some water.

"Ooops," he said, looking at Cassems, "I got the wrong bloke." His voice was husky probably from spending all day in the water.

Morris Yates swung around to find himself face to face with the boy.

"Shit'" he exclaimed. Then again, louder, "Shit!"

Cassems held his hand out, as they all trod water in a circle.

"Morris, I'd like you to meet Marty."

Just then Liz and Denny surfaced next to the two men.

Liz looked at Marty. "I told you to aim more to the right."

After introductions and apologies, the five circled around in an odd standoff. Ducking waves to hold their positions.

"You jumped a lot if you didn't think it was anything serious," Marty commented, looking at Morris.

"Leave it Marty," said Cassems.

Liz saved the situation.

"I'm mightily impressed at meeting you Mr Yates. Famous architect, designer of the Leo place and you've even got a waterfall named after you."

Morris looked at Cassems.

"I took them there as a reward for being outstanding models," Cassems said by way of explanation. "Besides how secret can the place stay?"

"We'd never tell anyone," Denny offered.

Morris turned to the small boy.

"It's okay Denny, I don't want to burden you with such an onerous responsibility."

"All the same," said Denny, "my lips are sealed on the matter." He drew the zip shut across his mouth to demonstrate his sincerity.

The five swimmers spent the next hour catching waves. The Brandy children took it upon themselves to critique each effort by the two adults.

"No, this one's too fat. No lift."

"The energy in a wave is in the top, you've got to dive deeper."

"You left your run too late."

"Gotta tuck in under the head there Morris."

"Not bad. I'd have made it to the shore on that one."

When challenged to put some of their bravado and commentary to the test they all caught wave after wave and swam like dolphins.

Marty got Morris again with a leg grab, with almost the same reaction.

Finally, insulted, injured and desperate, Cassems and Morris shoved all three children under a giant wave as it rose and then rode it to shore in triumph.

They stood and watched as Liz and Marty popped up alongside them, spitting out water. Denny was not there.

"Oh hell," said Morris, "you don't think I've drowned the little tacker do you?" he asked, looking anxiously at his friend.

They scanned the water then noticed Denny at the side walking toward them. He'd still caught the wave.

On shore the children spent some minutes standing with their heads bowed dribbling water out of their noses.

The men were amazed. Every time it seemed there could be no more, they would let forth another gush.

Morris looked at Cassems and shrugged.

"All kids do it. Hollow heads perhaps?"

Finally, they stood upright.

Now came the awkward bit.

"Well, we're off now," Cassems offered, "see you guys later."

Not that easy.

"We want to come." said Denny.

"Promise we'll be quiet," added Marty.

"We like Mr Yates," put in Liz.

"Please call me Morris," said Morris. "Look, I think you should get yourselves dry. Where are your towels?"

Cassems made note to tell Morris that the Brandy kids wore nothing else except their shorts and had rarely been seen with a towel hence the white layers of salt he often noticed on their air-dried bodies.

They stood in a circle, awkward and silent for a moment.

It was Denny, looking up at the two tall men who delivered the coup de gras. "Don't you like us?" he asked.

Cassems managed some small retrieval of dignity by extracting a departure time from his three small guests.

They sat on the outdoor deck piled together in their monkey group.

They took turns to question Morris about his life and his association with Cassems. Cassems was preparing tea and cake, hoping the architect wouldn't be caught out and reveal some tasty sample of their days of chasing women and being unsavoury idiots.

As he approached the group, tray in hand, he heard Morris trying some counter questioning to try to put the guests off their tack.

"So why does the universe exist?"

There was a pause while Cassems put down his tray.

"Well, we need somewhere to live," suggested Marty.

He emphasised the 'somewhere' as if it was obvious that the universe existed for the sole purpose of providing the kids with accommodation.

Morris looked up at Cassems handing out cake.

"I'm done, you take over."

"Yeh," said Liz, "Tell us about that time in New York with Cassandra?"

Cassems glowered at his mate.

"How the hell did that come up?"

Morris looked perplexed.

"I don't know, it just did. They're tricky little bastards."

Liz looked hurt. "Bastards?"

"Well not literally. But I'm not taking tricky back."

Cassems settled into a seat.

"Oh I agree. They're evil. You kept your adult otherworldliness for a couple of minutes. Now I've got four bloody kids sitting on my lounge."

"My kids are still kids," countered Morris. "I have a five and a three year old who appear to be five and three."

"They're so young," said Liz, "we're much more mature."

Denny sat picking lumps of spilled cake off his stomach then announced. "This cake is salty."

Everybody stopped. Marty wet a finger and ran it across his brother's stomach then tasted. "You're salty," he said, "You're coated." He looked round with a half-smile triumphing in his deductive powers.

So the afternoon went. A rambling, disjointed collection of verbal thrust and parry as the two men sought to evade the relentless Brandy style of questioning, interspersed with tangential bursts of irrelevant facts and conjecture.

At one stage when their backs were turned Morris and Leo realised the children were missing.

"They've gone?" queried Morris. "They didn't even say goodbye."

"No," Cassems raised his finger skyward. "They'll be up in your tower. They love checking out the neighbourhood from up there. Keeping an eye on things. Knowing what's going on."

"Do you ever use it?"

Cassems looked guilty. "Not really. Don't want to know. It looks great though. The house wouldn't be complete without it."

When the children returned, Morris asked, "So, what did you see?"

"The world," said Liz. "It's still there." She paused. "Waiting for us."

At 4pm Cassems demanded the Brandy children depart as agreed. By 4.35pm he had achieved this delicate manoeuvre and actually watched them trudge up to the top of the cliff path and disappear.

They had wanted to take the inland path that led to the front door but Cassems ever wary, had seen the possibility of them doubling back. This way he had a fair chance that they would stay gone.

He walked back from the balcony and looked at Morris.

"Well, you met them after all."

It was an undisclosed question.

"I don't know what to make of them," Morris said. He shrugged. "They're not precocious as such. From my limited experience that brings with it a certain objectionable cockiness. And there was none. I thought they were quite nice kids."

He paused and looked at the artist.

"Could be you're not used to kids and you're finding a group of young people charming when they're just ordinary kids."

"Seriously," said Cassems, "you consider 'them' average kids."

Cassems eyed his guest intensely. He lifted his arm halfway

to a gesture then seemed to change his mind.

"Don't go away," he said.

He lifted a finger in a sort of Papal movement. He walked up past the kitchen into the corridor behind. Shortly afterward Morris could hear the noise of a search.

Some minutes later Cassems returned with an assortment of items. He laid them on the table.

"This," he stated, "is research. Material that I didn't plan to ever show to anybody. Except that I didn't know you were going to turn up and didn't count on your level of naivety. Come and take a look."

The two men had before them a series of photos.

"I printed these out on my own printer," Cassems explained. He pointed to the first large image.

"Here are these ordinary kids sitting down the bottom of the cliff at the edge of the beach, surrounded by and patting black wallabys."

"So?" Morris looked again. "Wallabies often become that friendly. They posed for you."

Cassems grew a little agitated.

"They didn't pose for any of these shots. You can see it's a tele lens. I was skulking around like some dirty old man taking the photos. They had me intrigued. That mob of wallabys have been in this area for some time. Blacks are solitary, not usually in a mob and this lot are skittish they don't go near humans."

He pulled another image out. It showed the Brandy children sitting on rocks near the surf. Next to them on the rocks were some birds. One bird was perched on the girl's knee. Another stood gazing about from the top of Marty's head.

"Sooty Oystercatchers." Cassems finger stabbed the print.

"Amiable birds, often see them down on the beach. They will poke around near you but not get that close, sit on your head? Never."

Cassems slid a dark, dim print from the pile.

The children were sitting together in the heath. It must have been on the slope at the far side of the beach. The camera was looking down on them. They each cradled small black furry objects.

Morris Yates peered. "What's happening here?" He sounded more subdued.

Cassems paused with a slightly triumphant intake of breath before the reveal.

"They .... are each holding a bandicoot. It's dusk, hence the poor light."

"Oh come on," said Morris peering again.

"I swear." Cassems pulled out several more prints. "I watched them for half an hour, till it was too dark to see. No mistake. Bandicoots are solitary and timid. They have three. Three that will sit on their laps."

Morris Yates went back over the prints. He examined each one in turn. He looked at Cassems.

"You couldn't have faked these. You're not that good on a computer."

Cassems grunted. "Of course I didn't. To what end?"

"Then," said Morris, "that's weird, odd, amazing .... alien? I can't attempt to explain any of what I see here."

He looked again.

"But," he added, "you've said that these kids have this almost magical ability to sneak up on you, know what's going on around them. If what you've told me is accurate, they

must have known you were there, watching them."
Cassems felt a slight involuntary tingle on his neck.
He stared at the images. It had not occurred to him! His
friend had a point.

CHAPTER 25

The Plot

Deborah Kent is seated at her desk, surrounded by the
accumulation of unread, unwanted mail and papers, left on
her desk while she was not there to defend its inviting empty
spaces. On her screen is a vast line of email traffic that has
similarly built up.

"Deborah darls. When did you get back?"

"Hi Lyn. About five minutes ago."

"Good, I haven't been ignoring you then."

The two journalists sit and chat. Early morning, not a rush
period. They started life at the 'Herald' together and have
remained slight rivals and respected friends ever since.

Deborah has a triangular nameplate on her desk. It says
'Clark's Daughter'. Lyn's odd sense of humour. A past
birthday gift.

Idle gossip takes place. Apparently, Doug and Jackie are an

item. Joe Mitcham is being given a new sports column, the coffee shop has introduced a great new light noodle salad, lunch menu. Max Ghent smiled at some people in the lift on Friday taking his annual smile record up to seven.

"Must be the time of the season," Deborah quipped, "gets to us all in holiday times."

"No, actually, I think it's the latest online figures. Sudden rush of people signing up and paying their money. We may have a future in journalism yet babe. Just that it will be electronic and yesterday's news will happen in seconds rather than days."

"I can live with that. I think I can live with that. I don't know?"

Lyn paused. "I heard your friend Georgie has moved on." She paused again.

"Or am I out of line?"

Deborah looked straight at Lyn.

"Hardly a secret round here. Actually, I moved on. Not sure where I'm at but that just wasn't my scene. Georgie is a fabulous person but you know, I think even she's not sure."

"Good for you," said Lyn, "if you ever do work it all out be sure to let me know."

Both women gave a snort of laughter.

Lyn grabbed her friend's wrist.

"Oh, oh, guess what, our little mate Lyle is onto something. He approached me last week, asked if I'd show Max some photos. Said I was one of the few people he could trust. Isn't that sweet? Anyway, the photos are from a hike he did in his break at some National Park down south."

"National Park shots, sounds so exciting," said Deborah.

"Ah but wait." Lyn held up a finger. "The photos are tele lens

shots of some kids having a skinny dip in a rainforest pool.
He was cutting through the top of a ridge, heard the noise
and thought he'd take some shots."

"Lyle better be careful he doesn't get a tap on the shoulder
from the authorities," Deborah added.

"Yeh," said Lyn, "but that wouldn't even occur to Lyle, you
know what a complete innocent he is. So, when he'd got back
from his days in the wilderness he showed them to a mate
of his in the local tourist centre with a view to making a few
dollars. Naive Lyle again. The guy actually liked the shots.
Another worry. I guess they don't have as many hangups
down there or the local tourist guy has some issues. Anyway,
he said they weren't sharp enough for their 'needs'.

Then just as Lyle is leaving the tourist guy looks at the
photos again and points out a figure lying on the slope above
the pool. He says he'd swear the person in the photo with
the naked kids is Leo Cassems, you know the famous artist.
Says he lives down that way."

Lyn leans closer. Her voice drops.

"Well, now Lyle smells a story and a bit of kudos. His big
break. A man taking some kids for a swim is nothing but Leo
Cassems hanging around with some naked kids, now that's a
story. Sordid and imminently nasty.

I spoke to Max on Lyle's behalf. Max says as long as we
can prove that it is Leo Cassems we can beat it up into
something. Down and out artist, on the skids, dubious and
questionable conduct around small children. Lyle's all full of
himself, thinks he's on a winner."

Lyn pursed her lips and raised her hands, palms up.

"Anyway, I'd say Lyle needs to do a lot of research. I told
him so. For a start, they could be Cassems' own kids. If the

photos are blurry it could all backfire. It could turn out to
be somebody else. You know Max with his publish and be
damned approach. If the paper gets sued again it will be Lyle
who's out the door unemployed and destitute."
Lyn then pressed on with more urgent matters. Her love life,
her dog, the play she saw last week. Finally, she stopped.
"Okay, I talk too much. Gotta do some work anyway. Good
you're back. Want to try the 'light' lunch around 12.30?"
Deborah, distracted said, "Yeh, sure, let's give it a go."
Lyn stopped.
"What?"
"Hey listen sister. Be careful with your helping Lyle and his
little plan for stardom. If he does make a mess of it you could
get swept up in the 'consequences'."
"Fair point. I'm staying away from him. I've done my charity
bit for this month. He's on his own. As I told him, he'd better
research the whole thing to death before he makes a move.
See you at lunch."

CHAPTER 26

Lyle and Leo

Up ahead Lyle can see Deborah Kent's rear as he follows it
in his headlights. He smiles to himself. A very nice little rear
he concedes. He is a little nervous. No, he is very nervous.
The woman in the SUV in front of his small car is leading
him along an unsealed bush road. It is late in the afternoon.
They are back in the territory he hiked in his holidays
though not any section that is familiar. He should be grateful.
Since finding out about his scoop story Deborah has been
seriously helpful and encouraging. He has put her on the top
of his most trusted journalistic colleagues, even above Lyn.
Lots of research has revealed the up and down career of his
subject. His paintings are legendary. Lyle even likes them
and Cassems appears to be an alright sort of chap. His past
is scattered with some quite interesting affairs. Not the
sort of modus operandi of a potential child botherer. It is

a slightly nagging issue in Lyle's mind but a story like this
can't be derailed by sentiment. Lyle is aware of the ethical
balance of his craft and how it must be skewed to succeed.
The key to his story being a winner is proving the man in the
photos is, in fact, Leo Cassems and it is here that Deborah
has been most helpful.
"There's only one way you're going to settle this Lyle," she
tells him. "Front the man, look him in the eye, then you'll
know. You'll have your story."
And she has convinced him that this is the way to get his
proof. The glowing byline in his future drives him on.
"Tell you what, I've got a spare day on Friday. We know
where he is. I'll go with you. Use some ruse that we're doing
a little piece on his great works. Even if he tells us to get lost
you'll have seen him. That will probably be enough." Damn,
this girl is clever.

He has to give Deborah her due, he would never have
found his way to Leo Cassems' house but with her uncanny
navigation skills. Here they are walking along a shaded green
track that winds around a slope to a small wooden bridge
and an impressive oversized wooden door.
"This has to be it," Deborah whispers. "It's the only house
anywhere, far as I can see."
Their footsteps echo slightly on the little bridge. To the left,
Lyle can see a huge wooden deck stretching out over the
bush slope. With its heavy sandstone foundations, the house
is large, bulky and strong. It cries out 'artist in residence.'
Deborah is already rapping on the door with an iron knocker
in the shape a kangaroo head. She seems fearless.
It is now that Lyle realises he is shaking. Hopefully not

enough for his companion to notice.

No sign of life emanates from the house. Deborah tries again, giving the knocker a severe pounding. This time it produces noise from inside and approaching steps. "Jesus Christ," is thundered from behind the door. They wait.

The door launches open and there stands a large, unhappy man. Lyle is almost certain it's the man in his photos. "What?" he snarls.

Deborah is immediately into the patter about wanting to do a piece on Leo Cassems' past work and his place in the country's art establishment. The man just stands there glowering. Lyle tugs at Deborah's sleeve in an attempt to beat a retreat. An awkward silence where Lyle considers running. But no, the man is looking them over. Lyle can hear his heart beating. Still the silence. Then Leo Cassems shrugs, says "What the hell," and ushers them in.

Lyle passes under his arm holding the door and thinks it will be good to destroy this rude man.

It takes a little over an hour for Lyle Bennett to get drunk, be charmed, laugh a lot, feel accepted and important, call Mr Cassems 'Leo' and completely dismiss his scoop story.

A story he has already 'confessed' to the artist.

"No," says Lyle Ghent accompanied by a nervous laugh, "It wasn't Leo Cassems. Probably just some guy with his kids. Not to worry."

Cassems doesn't need coaxing, the Brandy family, the children and their part in his new series of works and their swim in the forest pool are all part of the story Leo Cassems unfurls as they sit about on the wooden deck. It is a magical tale and Lyle is soaking it up as a sponge in warm water.

Cassems' joy, his enthusiasm, wash about the room in a tide
of emotion that collects the trio and carries them along.
What wonderful people these Brandys must be. He feels as if
he knows them all.
The wine is good and there's a meal. Then some Brie and
dates and brandy. They chat as erudite adults and equals.
Lyle realises he knows a bit about art and he likes it.

Then comes the moment that will be one of the most
memorable in Lyle Bennett's life. Leo Cassems puts an arm
around the young journo's pencil-like shoulders and ushers
him into the back room studio full of paintings waiting for
collection to his new exhibition.
"It's not all of them," Cassems explains, "about one third.
The rest are already there. I know you'd like to write this up
but I appeal to you as a professional, can you embargo this
until the exhibition. I promise I'll give you an exclusive tour
on the night. You are coming aren't you?"
Lyle is entranced. He dares to touch one or two of the
canvases. He sees the eyes of the child in the undergrowth,
the sinewy bodies on a tree's branches. He is surprised when
Marty's sly grin echoes from the dense undergrowth. There
in the silky curl of ocean waters Liz slides in the halos of
light and dark that is Cassems work.

When they finally leave with much heartiness, handshaking
and camaraderie, Lyle is transformed into a slave of the arts.
It will be a lifelong and quite fulfilling role.
"By the way Lyle, it occurs to me that in the wrong hands
the story of these kids, beautiful moments like the day at
the pool and so on, could be easily misinterpreted by some

hack with a view to some minor glory or a quick buck. I'd
appreciate your complete professional integrity regarding
passing on any information that could hurt them in any way.
Their choice of anonymity or not will be theirs to make."
They shake hands one more time with Lyle nodding
vigorously.
"God knows what I'd do to anybody who did harm them."
It is all unnecessary. Lyle is already a keeper of the Brandy
secret.

Along the path, approaching their cars, Deborah lets out a
snort.
"You've got the bastard," she chuckles, "God, I didn't think
it would be so easy. What a deviate. He even told us all
the sordid details. Lyle this story is going to rip him apart.
You're gonna be a star old mate."
Lyle is struck by immobility and lack of speech as one.
"What?" he finally manages, "what!?" His voice is so high it
squeaks.
"I said ...."
Lyle rises to his maximum height in the moonlight. "Are you
insane Debbie? The man is a genius, he's ...... he's a bloody
saint. The only story I'm ever going to write about him will
be so dripping with praise and admiration I'll probably be
chucked off the press for making readers sick." Lyle felt he
had made his point. He waited.

Deborah elbows him gently in the ribs.
"Those paintings were rather magical." She pauses. "I was
just having a little light moment there Lyle. You know, one
journalist to another. If you'd decided to pursue your story

after what we've seen and heard and eaten, I was going to
kill you and bury you next to that tree you're standing under.
Call me Debbie again and it could still happen."
"That's all right then," said Lyle, fingering his neck, looking
at the stars.
At the main road, Deborah puts her hand out the window
and indicates for them to stop.
"Listen," she says, "You can make your own way back to
Sydney from here. Seeing I'm down this way I'm going to
surprise a friend I haven't seen for while."
Lyle jumps out his car. "Do me one favour before you go?"
"What would that be Lyle?"

Pulled off down a small service track the two journos crouch
over a cleared patch of earth.
"You don't have to do this Lyle."
"No, I want to. Once it's done there can be no going back.
No more temptation. It's over and I can move on." Lyle takes
a book of matches from his pocket and strikes a match.
His first two attempts fail and just as Deborah is about to
snatch the matchbook from him he manages to light the
pile of photos and roll of colour negative film piled on the
ground.
They stand back and watch the brief burst of flames as the
small fire flares and then dies away to ashes.
"There it's done."
"No going back now, Lyle. I guess you've really found some
closure. All the same, you should buy yourself a digital
camera. A decent one. They're so much better and easier to
use. Sharper, no messy processing. Didn't know you could
still get film."

Lyle winces.

"You're right. It was my Dads. He had a whole outfit. Lot's of lenses. Maybe I will retire it all now. "

She gives the young man a quick hug.

"You old sentimentalist. Hey, if it makes you happy, keep using it. Eventually, there'll be nobody to process the film you can't get anyway, then the decision is made for you. See you back at the office. Be good."

As Lyle drove away into the night he wondered if the rumours about Deborah were true. What would have transpired if they'd booked into some motel together?

He liked to think that something may have happened despite the rumours.

Then his mind moved onto shiny new cameras.

A half hour later Cassems answered a gentle knock at his door. Deborah stood there in the moonlight. She looked soft, with her white shirt and khaki dress.

"Even the sandals," said Cassems.

"Pardon?"

"Nothing. An artist thing. That was terrifying," Cassems said. "Fate. God, if he hadn't known you. I dread to think ... How can I thank you?"

"Where did you hide Morris?"

"He's in the city chatting to Government people with big budgets."

Deborah looked at Cassems.

"Well, don't think of what could have happened. You now have a friend for life in Lyle Bennett. At first, I thought you were a hell of an actor then I understood. Everything you

said about this whole experience was passion. No acting. I really get you Leo."
Cassems stepped forward and took the woman in his arms. He hugged her tightly, in gratification for all she had done. Their hug did not let up.

CHAPTER 27

At The Gallery

Georgie Little was almost in tears. She told Cassems of
her happiness as she appeared and disappeared many times
while people poured through the gallery doors and into the
rooms. Cassems was amused, no he was delighted. If Georgie
was happy then life would be much simpler.

Her business nose was more highly attuned than her
appreciation of art but Cassems concluded that the balance
was in his favour.

The artist was amazed when his agent booked the biggest
gallery in the city. A monster of a place. Room after giant
room. All creamy white. A grand old building, used for civic
functions when not showing art collections.

He was more amazed at his output. His work filled the
place. Admittedly, one room was crammed full of framed
sketchbook pages that Georgie had 'acquired'. She had also

found a number of discarded canvases still in the workup
stage and cleverly added a little story to each about the
creative process. Then, to make them more desirable she
had marked them not for sale. They filled a side room.
Normally Cassems would have been annoyed at such actions
without his consent but the stories were quite sympathetic
and somehow made a point. Works in raw form had a certain
intrigue even he knew that.
He was more watchful of Georgie's mood for another reason.
Did she know about Deborah? If so, she showed no signs.
He dared not ask her.
The man was a coward in matters of the heart.
Not completely sure that the previous relationship was no
more. Why were women so enigmatic?

Lyle Bennett arrived quite early and Cassems walked him
through the rooms as promised. He found the young man's
enthusiasm and interest quite refreshing in the rather false
world of art. He talked freely about the background and
reasoning behind a number of the works before noting that
he was, after all, talking to a journalist and should be a little
circumspect. He left Lyle with a glass of champagne and a
handful of canapes, staring into a forest, at the three Brandy
children in a little lost group at a distance from the viewer
deep in amongst the trees. Lost or exploring? It was hard to
say. Bennett stared at the painting. It had a slightly Victorian
old world charm.

The pulse of people and chatter washed over Cassems.
He turned from the gushing praise of yet another art
dilettante to see Jennifer and Tom enter the gallery. They

were searching for him. In that brief moment, before their eyes met, he was able to observe this elegant, gentle, woman and the man she loved so much.

She wore a filmy grey-green dress that suited her perfectly. It was the first time he had seen her in high heels.

The transformation to chic was effortless. Tom looked surprisingly neat in a jacket and blue shirt that had a slightly, dishevelled way about it. Cassems recognised a fellow artist. Tom looked young again. Perhaps it was a curse for him. Remarkably his limp was almost gone. The man must be purposeful in his quest to overcome the injury. He had apparently not even considered there could be a permanent impairment.

Jennifer saw him. He felt a guilt he would continue to carry as he looked across and smiled at the couple. Tom lifted his hand in a salute.

The children were on their way he discovered. Logistics had required that they come directly from their school. A taxi had been arranged.

After some pleasantries, Jennifer and Tom immersed themselves in the paintings. For them, it was a first viewing. A chance to decide on the depth of the whole prolonged process that involved so much of their recent lives. Cassems wished he could be nearby to listen in and answer the question. Did these people like what he had done?

Instead, he idled about engaging in frivolous banter with various patrons. He was encouraged by the genuine interest from the art lovers in the crowd as opposed to the art buyers who saw his name as an investment. Strangely, he thought, the latter category were a better gauge as to the success of this latest outpouring. Art had lost a lot of it's charm. It was now a business based less on talent and more on star quality and trends. It had the same insane, illogical ups and downs as the stock exchange.

Later he became aware of their presence in the building. He had no idea why he knew. He sought ways to move from room to room in the grand old place with its excellent lighting.

There they were, in their tight reliant group, off in a corner examining in some detail a section of rainforest from which their own eyes in acrylic, stared back at them.

Cassems watched, intrigued, trying to translate their reactions. To know that he had caught their soul and buried it so deep in the dark undergrowth. He was sure he would be able to tell. At times his eyes lost contact as various viewers made polite conversation. He answered as best he could while rudely staring over their shoulders and positioning himself to keep watching the Brandy children.

They were still handsome in their dark navy blue uniforms, with red piping and a crest on the pocket but the essence was bottled, hidden away. They existed now in an artificial world that restricted their natural energy. Cassems thought of caged birds meant to soar and chatter in coloured bursts through treetops, reduced to standing on a perch.

Morris Yates appeared briefly at his shoulder. He leaned close and whispered, "Are you watching them or are they watching you?"

Cassems smiled as his friend moved on into the crowd.

At a point in the rumble of art world gossip, inspection, comment and procession of meet the artist opportunities,

there came a sudden moment of peace. The scene about
Cassems shifted away. The tide briefly ebbed. He viewed
from afar the figures and props and paintings.
"My God," he thought, 'Nobody has asked about the
models."
A masterwork covering the walls of many rooms. A theme
that repeats in nearly every work yet not a word of inquiry
as to who or what inspired such an effort.
And they were here. Albeit unrecognisable. Cleverly
disguised as schoolchildren. There were other children
about of course but did people think he created them?
Cassems moved to a smaller side room. The three were
there, once again examining at close range the paint that
held an image of a leg caught by light as the rest of the figure
of Liz held a mysterious presence in the shadow of palm
fronds. Her gaze in this painting was elsewhere. The girl on
the canvas looked away into the canvas world, searching for
something that even Cassems could not name. They were
fascinated by the mechanics of each work as much as the
image itself viewed from a distance.
As he watched, Marty turned and their eyes met. The boy
smiled across the room in a mix of warmth and genuine
excitement. Cassems enjoyed the conspiracy of the moment.
There was the answer to his concern. His children were still
there. Time may have slightly moved the figures on the stage
but the play continued to be written.

And when they finally emerged from the gallery side rooms
and entered the main hall, there before them hung Cassems'
biggest work. A giant depiction of the hole on the beach
containing their three sleeping figures.

They stood for ages, just looking, not moving, breathing in
their existence.
Cassems was pleased. The painting was up high. For once
they would have to settle for the whole image. And it
appeared to work.

There was a burst of light. A flash. Deborah stood to the side
of the Brandy children with her press camera. She walked
over to Cassems.
"If you could have seen their faces in profile. It's a photo
you'll want to have. Did I spoil the moment?"
The children continued to stare.
"Nope," said Cassems.
Almost without consultation, they had agreed the children
would be protected, not revealed if at all possible.
Cassems hoped the Brandy kids agreed. He sensed they did.
It would suit them more to have the secret than not.
Lyle Bennett caught his eye at one stage and slid his eyes
to the kids. They both gave a knowing nod. He must have
spent some time seeking them out in the crowds. It seemed
to please the young journalist immensely. Cassems had a
feeling the trust would not be broken.

By 8.45pm the crowds were thinning. Gerald Moore, art critic
and general bon vivant deemed it time to parley with the
artist.
Gerald had been regaling a group of followers with an
oft-repeated tale of another well-known artist, now deceased.
The story involved the early days when the man had been
a struggling newcomer. Gerald had visited his studio and
found the man just getting by, living almost exclusively on

tins of pilchards because they were the cheapest food at the supermarket. He had used the empty tins to mix his paints. At his first exhibition a number of viewers had commented on the slightly fishy smell in the rooms. The artist was concerned but Gerald had assured him that the secret of the fishy paint would be safe as long as either of them was alive. Cassems didn't mind the man, despite his rather grand approach to social interaction he did know his subject and was not swayed by anything outside his own perceptions. He had always been a supporter of Cassems' work with the exception of a last showing nearly four years before. It was a halfhearted effort by an artist who had lost interest and Gerald Moore was quite cutting in his assessment.

They had not spoken since.

"Dear boy," said Moore, vigorously shaking Cassems' hand. "Where have you been? Welcome back." He paused. "No, not welcome back. You've moved on. Progressed. It's taken me a while to come to grips. Historians will no doubt name this new period you've embarked on. But ....." he paused again, "a triumph."

Members of the crowd had moved closer to catch the valued Moore opinion.

"Thank you, Gerald. That's good to hear. You know ...."

Gerald Moore cut him short. He urgently placed a grip on Cassems forearm.

When excited he tended to run away at the mouth. Cassems had no problem with praise.

"What transformed you? I had heard terrible tales of your woes. Melancholia, drunkenness, whoring. "There goes a great artist," I said. "Dear, dear.... Now here you are. These brooding, lush forests and these children. Like, like they

are part of the trees and plants. The earth itself. They add
a marvellous magic. You can't be categorized. You're a
romantic, wrapped in impressionist/expressionist layers.
An abstract with art nouveau undertones. What inspired this
all?" Gerald swept his arm about in vaudevillian gesture. Was
the question rhetorical?

Cassems briefly considered calling Jennifer and Tom and the
children over. It seemed obvious that questions would be
asked and they would be tracked down. He deemed it better
to reveal them now in a controlled manner. They were in his
line of sight, chatting and accosting a waiter for the complete
contents of his tray of snacks. Then Gerald Moore swung
his arm back, almost losing a fob watch and chain from his
elaborate waistcoat.
"And all built around these marvellous creations, these
fantasy children you've managed to conjure up. To populate
your world with these beautiful, impossible creatures.
A genuine triumph dear boy and I will say so. Many times
over."
Moore leaned closer to Cassems and whispered. "I've
purchased one. A smaller work from out the back."
"Oh God no, Gerald, please, consider it a gift."
Moore almost spat his reply.
"Never. You're an outrageously expensive bastard but I will
not have my integrity sullied by bribery. Say no more about
it."
Gerald paused.
"I believe the National has dibs on that."
He gestured over his shoulder at the giant canvas of the hole
in the sand.

He added, "Among others."

Then he smiled and looked into Cassems eyes.

"It's so good to have you back, Leo. I've really missed you.
I like the new you even more. A most wonderful evening all
round.."

He turned away with a flourish. Cassems watched the
departing figure, almost floating out of the room with several
friends in tow.

Toby Whitby, an up-and-coming critic/dealer from a rival
publisher looked at Cassems.

He nodded after the departing Gerald.

"What he said."

They both laughed and nearly spilt their drinks.

"I'd change a few words so it looks original, Toby."

They laughed again.

He felt an odd mix of emotion. The National wanted his
painting. It would hurt to let it go. It meant more than he had
realised.

The evening was complete. And Liz, Marty and Denny were a
fantasy. Too amazing to be real.

CHAPTER 28

At The Dancing Frog

At 9.00 pm, with the gallery to close at 9.30 pm, Cassems
found the Brandy family preparing to depart.
"Oh no," he said, "you can't escape that easily. I have a huge
debt to pay. It should start tonight."
He insisted on buying them dinner. Perhaps the genuineness
of his invitation convinced them. Georgie was heavily
involved in discussions with some people who were
mentioning rights, royalties and other matters. The
discussions appeared earnest and involved. Deborah had
been seconded by Georgie to help her and out of some past
loyalty decided to stay with the woman who was doing her
best to talk to three different people at once. She looked a
little sad at missing out and they quietly departed.
A short taxi ride with Denny and Marty hidden below the
window line to avoid the seat belt laws and they arrived

at 'The Dancing Frog'. The taxi driver accepted a small
additional fee for "risking his livelihood," with extra
passengers.

"That's okay Mr Leo Cassems," he said, "I love your work."
Cassems joined his party, glancing back at the departing taxi.
In a city where even taxi drivers often surprised you.

Shown in by a waitress they were seated at the back on
a garden terrace when they were confronted by a small,
intense Frenchman who punched Cassems repeatedly on the
arm. He positively purred as he introduced himself.
An impression of almost explosive bonhomie issued from his
very being.
"I couldn't get to the gallery tonight, my friend. I'll go later
in the week. It's better when there are less people about and
there's time to reflect. The word is out though. You are back
in favour. I knew you'd do it. Oh Leo, I'm very happy."

The menus were held tightly to his chest. He seemed to
know more than would have been immediately obvious
for a random restaurateur. He was, on a small mission of
enlightenment. It was as he updated the Brandy family with
tales of a school kid he knew, then a rough-living, dead beat
art school attendee named Leo who cleaned dishes at the
Frog for food, wine and some money, that a sizeable missing
part of Leo Cassems life appeared before them.
"Lonely boy," concluded the Frenchman without explanation.
He handed out the menus to all his guests.
Arnaud was proud of what his dishwasher had become.
He had three of his paintings. "No, not here, at home. If I
have them here some crazy bastard breaks in and steals the

painting. At home it is secure. I have an extremely big dog
as well. And he is an art lover like me. Nobody would live to
leave the premises."

He pauses, runs his fingers through Cassems lengths of black
hair. "Still do this, eh? What is wrong with your friends they
don't get my .... my witticisms. That dog joke is some of my
best material. Patrons have convulsed."

It is now that the Brandy family is sufficiently assured to
laugh as one.

"Ah," says Arnaud, "holding back, not sure, impolite to find
his craziness jocular. I love your friends."

He leaps round the table and grabbing their faces kisses all
five of the Brandy family on the lips. Finally standing back,
he punches Cassems' arm one more time. Then he snatches
the menus back.

"Don't look at these things. I will bring lots of fine stuff.
You just enjoy yourselves."

Tom watches the man heading back through his restaurant
snapping orders to his crew.

"Is he .... ?" Tom looks enquiringly.

"No, he's just French, excitable, you know. Married, to
Juliette over there. Two lovely, studious daughters. I slept
here a lot out the back. He loves food and art or art and
food. All the waiters will be art students. He sort of adopts
you. Dyes his hair though. I don't."

"Does he know about us? About the kids?"

"Yes, he does. When I moved down the coast I promised
him that I'd call him once a month. He said he didn't
care whether my life was shitty or fantastic I had to keep
him informed. To make up for not being a regular at his
restaurant. Underneath the happy frenchman facade there's

a man who knows art. Also a thouroughly decent and
kind being. So yes, I told him all about my visions of your
children. He understood straight away. Encouraged me to
pursue the whole thing. I had to bring you here tonight.
He wanted to see you."

True to his word Arnaud covered the table with selections of
incredibly rich French Provincial soups, bread, terrines, pies
and delicacies some of which he hinted contained parts of
animals that should not be mentioned to the children.
He insisted that the children also drink his favourite
cabernet merlot, pouring them generous glasses that soon
saw them slumped against the adults.
"It is my only regret about settling in this country," Arnaud
commented as he passed, "The local kids can't handle their
wine."

Cassems proposes a toast. He is slurred but functional.
"At risk of repeating myself. You people came into my life
and changed it. I was a perfectly content has-been. But
oh no, not good enough, you had to slip your beautiful,
delightful children into my line of vision and what do you
know - I was hooked. No more aimless walks on the beach
and getting inebriated by noon. I had a purpose again."
He stopped. Tom and Jenny were looking at him kindly as if
they were not sure what all the fuss was about.
"Anyway, you saved me. Please accept my sincere thanks
and endless gratitude."
His voice was thin. The man's eyes were filling up. Tom
shook his hand vigorously.
Jenny slid across to Cassems and hugged him. She then

pulled back and kissed his cheek and briefly kissed his lips.

"Enough," said Mr Cassems. "Been a hell of a journey for us all."

Rested against her father Liz watched the artist and her mother.

Arnaud saw them off with more zealous kisses and hugs. "So, just drop in anytime again unexpected, after ignoring me for a suitable period. Once I visit the gallery I will call you Leo and give you a full appraisal. I will not hold back out of loyalty and friendship. My words will be sincere and unbiased. Expect no favours."

"I would have it no other way, Arnaud."

The frenchman punched Cassems' arm one more time, said "Clever bastard," and left.

They took separate taxis. The Brandy group to their home and Cassems to his hotel.

The following weekend they would be back at the beach house for one last summer visit.

CHAPTER 29

On Trial

Leo Cassems, rediscovered, reinvigorated, sat on his deck
and stared up through the leaves of trees at the sky.
He saw the scene in sections. A mosaic of the mind.
Counted the colours and named the paints. Imagined filling
in the final details with a No.7 sable hair brush before
declaring it right.
He was pleased more than he had been in many years.
Yesterday Deborah had left to return to her job but not
before they had both admitted that they enjoyed being
together more than would be the situation if it were just
tedious lust.
They had slept together, cooked together, eaten together,
talked together, discussed great and trivial things and found
they both grew tired of cryptic crosswords very quickly.
"I think people who enjoy cryptics think of themselves as

a particularly clever and somehow a special breed when they're really just tedious."
Cassems looked at Deborah and said, "You just read my mind. How did you do that?"

In a fit of spontaneous gesturing at their parting, as Deborah returned to her work, Cassems had muttered some words whose general inference was that he'd be happy if their time together could become a more permanent and formalised arrangement.
Deborah had looked shocked.
"Oh God," he thought, "Wrong thing, too soon, too eager?"
Then she hugged him.
"How could I not adore somebody who could do that to the language," she said.
And so they briefly moved on with every intention of setting Cassems' arrangement in motion. And now Cassems lay back in his chair and smiled. He realised it was the first time in a large space of his recent life when he was not pondering the members of the Brandy family. Yet their essence continued. He had never given serious thought to a woman permanently in his life. Perhaps because he associated with the wrong women or possibly because he was a bit of a thoughtless bastard. Arnaud may be right? Here he was eagerly pursuing such an arrangement and in his most hidden moments pondering the ongoing possibilities of offspring and all that they had to offer.
Family? It was a word. Now it there, in his head.
"Bloody Brandys," he muttered loudly, then glanced about as if somebody may have heard.
He dozed, fitfully.

He dreamt. He was at school. In the long oak-lined corridor that led to the huge assembly room at the college. Boys walked in groups or pairs. He walked alone.

Boarders didn't fit in quite as well as the day boys. But there was more to it than that. Leo Cassems was a bit of an oddball. Said the wrong things, did odd things. The first two years had been a little easier with his brother in attendance. Now he had moved on. Gained acceptance into a city law firm. His parents were pleased in their conservative way.

Just as they were dismayed by their second child Leo.

He majored in the subjects that to them were of no use, arts, humanities, literature.

By the end of his fourth year at sixteen he had lost interest in all subjects and his exam results were poor. Sport no longer appealed and his on-field performances meant he failed to be selected for teams. Girls found him initially attractive and he gained further displeasure of the masters by being known to have lost his virginity at thirteen. His ongoing success in this area meant he was banned from the inter-school dances.

Now the crowd all headed along this endless corridor to the hall.

Cassems knew what was in store before he arrived. He could feel it coming. He reached the doorway. All the others were inside waiting for him. All the log-headed, knuckle-dragging, inbred sons of the leaders of commerce and industry who were at the school with no interest in learning or academic fulfillment. Just the old school tie and the connections that attendance brought. Both highly valuable assets once one moved into the family business.

While his parents had struggled to pay the fees, his

fellow students were flush with privileges and ostentatious lifestyles.

He could avoid it no longer. Cassems entered the hall.

In a jump he sat upright, looking about, re-orientating, returning to the present. Like any person awakened in such a way, Cassems glanced about to ascertain his position and ensure that he was alone.

He settled back. "Someday," he thought, "I'll find out what awaits me in that hall."

Leo Cassems was quite circumspect about his upbringing and schooldays. Even in interviews as his fame grew he managed to skirt the subject deftly and distract interviewers with counter-questions that put them off course.

He thought of Arnaud's off-hand comment at the restaurant. "Lonely boy." Nobody had picked up on that.

On one of his frequent days of truancy from the school existence, he had literally been sitting in the gutter of some chic, tree-lined inner-city street. A pile of charcoal sticks left from a small council fire had given him the chance to cover near ten metres of the concrete gutter with sketches, doodles and assorted graphics.

A small, dark-haired young man with a neat moustache had approached and stopped.

Wordlessly he leaned over and slowly examined the gutter workings each step bringing him closer to the perpetrator. Instead of the obvious question. "Why aren't you in school?" he said, "Mon dieu, you are good. So good!" He tugged the blazer. "You don't belong in this pissy establishment.

You belong in art school!"
Cassems had looked up at the man. The man with the
moustache smiled back and nodded as if agreeing with
himself.
"Ah," he said. "You know I'm right, don't you."
They sat for half an hour in the gutter discussing art.
Then the schoolboy was coaxed to the Frenchman's small
restaurant which occupied much less than the half a street
that it does today.
There he had a free meal and discovered that nothing in life
is free as he washed dishes with a guy called Colby Tennant.
Now a quite successful book illustrator.
Then, Colby was working his way through art school.
It took four months of incessant diplomacy, pleading
with parents, school discussions, art school discussions,
assessments and dinners for five at The Dancing Frog.
The five dinner participants, consisting of Leo Cassems'
parents, his brother, the restaurant owner, Arnaud, and
Leo Cassems himself were convened to discuss this crazy
concept that a sixteen-year-old schoolboy could somehow
be allowed to give up a very expensive education and throw
his lot in with Bohemians and ne'er-do-wells of the art world
on the absurd off-chance that he may be able to sustain
some sort of living from the creative process.
Needless to say, the person with the highest stake in these
discussions was the one who was allowed the least input.
Leo Cassems sat glumly while Arnaud's passion for art and
those that inhabited its precincts were battered against the
stoic logic of a good education, university, a worthwhile
diploma and a good job.
In the end, it was a factor that perhaps only the potential

artist himself could notice that won the day for a 'trial' at
art school. The school's complete indifference to losing this
no account student made the extraction from the old-boy
network and placement in a prestigious art school so much
easier.
Arnaud gave young Leo a job and he plunged into the limited
pallets and strictures of a first-year art student.
He paid Arnaud for the free family dinners by designing a
dancing frog that still adorns the building today. He paid him
again when fame arrived with several paintings.
He could never repay the faith of the man or the
understanding when first his parents died in quick
succession leaving debt rather than inheritance and within
a year his brother was taken by a drunk with a massive 4WD
on a twisty suburban street.
Incredibly distant relatives had sent flowers and
condolences to all three funerals but never appeared.
They only inquired as to his well-being and possible
remembrance of them when his fame and obvious wealth
brought him into the public eye. Cassems did not respond.
Not from any anger, just a mighty indifference.

Despite his fame, Leo Cassems had never heard from his
old school. Occasional meetings with former pupils brought
forth unsolicited comments. "I'm sure they're real proud
of you, y'know." As if the speaker knew something that
Cassems was not privy to.
It was not a weeping sore. After all he hated the place.
Academic curiosity.

On a whim, one winter's day he called in. It was not far out of his way in a visit to the city. Told the gatekeeper he was applying for a teaching job.

In the vaulted entry hall he sat for a while soaking the ambiance. Students moved past with the studied indifference he knew so well.

Nobody asked or cared about who he was or why he was on the premises.

He mused over the records of former student heroes. Giants of commerce and industry, generous benefactors. At the end of the mighty main corridor leading to the big hall, near a door next to the stairs he found one of his smaller paintings. Not one of his better works but nicely framed at least. Underneath a brief outline of his life together with a press photo from a few years back.

Other school photos of Leo Cassems had him circled. A tiny figure in a class of twenty. Another showing him with arms folded in a football team. No mention of his early departure from that same team or the school. The reader was left to assume that he had successfully completed his studies and that they had given him a wonderful grounding for his later success.

With the great hallway empty he took hold of a small piece of timber filigree near the stairs and broke it off. He placed it in his pocket and left. Somebody would be blamed for the damage.

He still had the little ornate curved piece. It sat on a shelf with the lighter broken timber exposed. Periodically he would notice it and smile.

Only one person had ever asked of its origins. Cassems had told him the whole story. He expected Charlie Coulson to be dismayed that he had damaged some fine timberwork but the old man was highly amused. He understood.

Leo Cassems
Diary note
Don't know about this. This girl, this woman, this Deborah.
Former sexual experimenter. Morris would say she's after my money. She can drink a bottle or two.
Doesn't smoke. Tick.
Enjoys and creates good conversation. Tick.
Intelligent but not overbearing. Tick.
Lets me be wrong. Tick.
Athletic - can outlast me. Grudging tick.
Doesn't crowd me. Tick.
Damned fine cook. A prerequisite. Tick.
Likes to be alone. Tick.
I love being in bed with her. Tick.
(As opposed to others I have just liked screwing and couldn't wait to be rid of ...)
Negatives .... haven't spotted any .... Tick.
I'd like to see a lot more of Deborah.
Why am I feeling a touch of guilt here. Not Georgie as it happens. She is unperturbed. Could she have set the whole thing up? Rumours abound that she has found another.

Should be seeing the Brandy lot tomorrow or next day. I have mixed feelings. Want to see them but then they will go and we will move toward Autumn. When they come again it will be different. There is little I can do.

I have one more gift. Bit presumptuous. Deborah's idea. Took some driving to find a kennel. A Weimaraner pup. Got a collar and lead. Quiet but playful little fellow with huge feet. In some burst of bravado I had the name Milo engraved on a brass disk for the collar.

So, with no warning, I present these people with a dog, which they are obliged to keep and look after. And in an added insult I have already named the animal.

How could they fail to be pleased.

They can always change the name - Just thought it looked like a Milo. The moment Deborah mentioned dogs I knew it had to be a Weimaraner. In a way the breed sums up the family. (I guess only those who have ever met one would know what I mean.)

I have a series of images in my mind. The three children and the dog caught in mid-flight running across the sand. An instant companion. Dogs always listen and they don't interrupt.

PS Dropped Morris at the airport. He swears he'll be back soon with his family, to stay. Can't say I believe him, can't say I don't.

As we sat having a coffee before his flight he told me of a conversation. At the gallery opening night he'd come upon the Brandy children looking into one of my jungle paintings. He asked them how they felt about being blended into the landscape. He thought it a light-hearted comment. Liz had answered.

"Nature experiments endlessly," she had said. "Humans are just another experiment after all. It carries no guarantees."
He looked at her for any hint of insincerity. When he found none he kissed her on the cheek and moved on.

CHAPTER 30

A Proposal

Marty and Denny are on a mission. Their parents are
asleep in the late afternoon light. They feel odd. Just the two.
Distantly ahead, slightly blurred by sea spray and heat haze
their sister Liz is crossing the back of their beach.
She is purposeful, making her way directly for the path to
the clifftop.
The boys feel lost. Their constant companion, the third cog
in of their wheel has struck out alone. Feigning sleep on the
back verandah couch they watched through slit eyes as she
slid away.
She is barefoot of course but wearing a strange filmy fairies
costume with wings. They had not seen it since a school
version of Midsummer Night's Dream about two years ago.
Why had she left them? They have a feeling they were
intruding. She must be going to Leo's house but why would

she want to see their friend alone? Why is she wearing a fairy costume? Keeping a very low stance they hid and watched her ascend the cliff path. At the top she paused as if making some final judgement, she looked about, out to sea, up at the birds then back down the cliff path and finally to the path away from the cliff. Momentarily there, she suddenly moved on and vanished.

At the base of the cliff path Marty and Denny could not go any further. Unspoken they were held back by a force of instinct.

They tarried for a moment then lay down on the beach grass below the line of the path.

In all this time they had not spoken. There seemed no need.

Cassems picked up a pencil and a pad. He had brewed coffee. On the deck a series of shadows began, cast by trees and the edge of the building.

He was contemplating life and how complex it could be. For the moment it was going through a less entangled period. With this new period came peace, although, because of his nature, Cassems still concerned himself with the more tiny aspects of interaction with others and their consequences. He sat staring at the mesh of massive eucalypts that screened his abode from parts the headland behind. In his mind, it was a wall though he knew not whether it kept intruders out or himself in.

The reviews had all been good. Sycophantic by some of the lesser lights, fair and balanced by those who knew the ropes. Lyle Bennett had written a delightful piece based on that of a novice happening upon Leo Cassems work for the first time. He used some of the insights imparted by Leo at the gallery but true to his word had not even approached any of the 'inside knowledge' he had on the subject. It showed a maturity that belied the quiet young man who had visited Cassems some weeks before.

The coffee was good. The man smiled as he realised that he had not brought out some snacks to enjoy with his coffee. The utter healthiness of Deborah was instinctively affecting his lifestyle already. Yet he was content. Entrapment, he thought. Nobody can warn you. Nobody can tell. Suddenly a person enters your life and you are okay with what transpires.

For a while Leo sketched a dark interpretation of the tree branches and leaves in the pad then found he had added a profile of Denny in the collection of lines. He stopped, wondered how they were. That Brandy family. The spark for it all.

Life has a way of throwing up heroes when needed. He certainly had his share.

He stared at the trees for some time and realised slowly that 'yes' he was currently quite happy. Life was good, if never calm, at least predictable again. Relaxed, he closed his eyes then for some reason opened them again.

Two sets of light, slim fingers moved across his eyes. Cassems amazed himself. He did not jump or even start. So trained, so drugged, so imbued by those kids and their ways that they had drained his response mechanisms.

"Am I guessing who?" he asked.

Silence.

"Liz," he said, "you have the longest fingers."

The fingers withdrew and light returned. Cassems turned. He expected to see Liz with her two partners standing behind him as usual with that annoying, benign, Giaconda smile of theirs.

Liz stood alone. With the low angle of the light she seemed odd, her expression purposeful and serious.

She walked from behind the chair and stood in front of him. It was now that he noticed she wore a strange filmy, pale-cream, translucent material. It was when he saw the wings he realised what it was that the girl wore. On the backlit deck he noted how strikingly pretty she was, if slightly odd. Every bit as beautiful and mysterious as her mother. She would command respect in years to come.

"You told me that fairies were your favourites," the girl said, her voice husky.

In a stylish bit of recall Cassems knew the conversation.

"Yes, I did," he said, "still stands." He shifted in his seat feeling he was missing something.

A silence came between them.

"Where?" he began, looking about, assuming that Marty and Denny were somewhere in the room.

For their benefit he added, in a stronger voice. "But the elves and others have their place, I mean it's a rich world and variation is what makes ...."

"I saw you that day," Liz said, her tone louder but flat and matter of fact.

Cassems felt his face warm. No, she couldn't mean?

She waited.

"I saw you together." She paused again.

"It's okay, you were both sad. About Tomdad. When you're

sad you don't think properly and things just happen. I was sad too so I watched you. You opened your eyes."

There was no malice in the girl's voice. Her calm demeanour conveyed some rationale that Cassems could not comprehend. He stayed silent. Horrified that his betrayal of Tom was not only known but had been observed. And by this young girl. His face reddened.

Liz moved forward. So strange in her fairy costume.

He now looked into those deep coloured pools of mystery that were the eyes of a Brandy child. For a while the girl simply stood, as if waiting, making up her mind about something.

Cassems felt decidedly uneasy. The closeness of this child. Her odd behaviour, her confession about his lapse with her mother.

This was not the situation he was used to with the girl.

He was about to speak , to say something, anything, when Liz became animated once more as if she had reached the next stage of her plan or play.

"You can't have my mother," she said. "Tomdad needs her. They're meant to be together for infinity."

Her voice was again quite loud.

She paused. Waited. Leaning in. Staring into the man's eyes.

Once again Cassems went to speak and was stopped by the next phase of the girl's message.

"So here's my deal. I know you need somebody. I mean you're that sort of person. Somebody to look after you and be yours. I have the answer."

She spoke as an adult would to an errant child. The words sounded slightly silly but also sad.

Cassems leaned back trying to put some small distance between himself and the body before him. The girl stepped forward, sat straddled on his knees and put her arms around his neck.
Cassems hesitently said, "What."
With her face out of focus in front of his she whispered in a rumbling husky voice to the side, to his ear, "You can have me instead."

CHAPTER 31

The Answer With No Question

Cassems considered himself a tough man. He had drunk and roughed it and had fights, done his bit of whoring and kept his sentimental side in balance for his whole life.
Now his face burned. He wanted to find some other interpretation of the girl's words. That this was all a setup. That the other kids were nearby and everything was an odd child joke.
He sat frozen by the enormity of what had been said. He ached for it not to be so.
His eyes filled. A tear slid out and made it's way down his cheek. The child on his knees kissed it away gently, looking supremely assured.
In getting to his feet he had to grab the girl to stop her hitting the floor.
Was he angry, confused, terrified?

He held her at length, hard and roughly by the shoulders.
He shook her. He bowed his head and almost cried.
"No, oh no, no." He could not get the words to form. They
came slowly, almost pleading.
"This is not right. You're ...... please don't spoil it. I want you
to be who you are for as long as possible."
He held her still by the shoulders. Perhaps gripping too
tight. She looked surprised. Not scared, not angry perhaps
shocked at the reaction she had caused. Not the one that
had rehearsed in her mind.
He shook her slowly as if not sure what to do with her, then
pushed her across the deck and down onto a lounge chair in
the studio.
"I thought you liked me," Liz murmured, wide-eyed.
"That hurt." She rubbed her shoulder.
Cassems was exasperated. He panted rather than breathed.
It was all wrong and he didn't want it to be.
He paused, now that the girl was seated and he was
standing. He paced in front of her, moving his hands about in
silent gestures.
This is a child, he thought. She has no idea of what she said.
A brave child full of loyalty.
Finally he found some words.
"Please don't be hurt Liz. Dear, dear girl. I love you more
than you can ever see. I love Marty and Denny and Jenny and
Tom. All of you. If there's a part of any person's life where
they would like to say, stop, take this piece and set it in some
unbreakable mould and I'll repeat it forever, then the times
since I met you and your brothers and your family, that
would be it."
The artist paused, hoping he made some sense.

"So you do love me," offered the girl.

"Yes," Cassems grasped the moment. "Of course, yes. But I'm incredibly selfish. I love what you are as well. Not what you were or will become, I love you all now and I don't want it to change." He almost yelled the last phrase.

"So alone, I'm not enough?" Liz now had a softness to her eyes. She had become a young girl again. Did she undertsand?

Cassems looked at her. Neat once more with her hands on her knees.

"You are a piece. But from a set that is rare and wonderful. And I've selfishly stolen into your world and taken what isn't mine. For that I'll be forever grateful Liz darling. If you thought today that there was a choice that you or I had to make, for the sake of your mother ……. Well, you were wrong and you were right. We were sad, that's all, you clever child. It was a way sharing our troubles.

There is no danger, no crisis. Your world and your wonderful parents are still complete and shall remain so. I offer no danger, only friendship."

Cassems looked at her again. Sitting on the couch in a fairy's outfit. Perhaps her twelve-year-old mind thought it was sexy.

"Someday there will be a person you'll want to say those words to again. Not some artist who was your neighbour once but somebody who'll mean a lot more to you."

Cassems thought, "and is currently about fourteen."

For a while the pair were silent, absorbing all the words. Cassems prayed that the sensibilities of a young, confused girl would not be troubled. Her immaturity might save them both. The sun began to cast large tree shadows across the deck.

Cassems looked out over the landscape he knew by sight and by touch. He finally turned and held out his arms.

Liz stood up from the lounge and walked into them.

The child he knew once more. They held each other tighter and longer not wanting it to end.

Cassems felt protective, fatherly in fact. He kissed the top of the girl's head.

Liz said quietly, "I'll never tell anyone about you and my Mum. What I know will go to my grave with me."

In a different time Cassems would have found the statement quite disarming and funny.

But now he just said, "I believe it will, dear Liz. And that's a long time."

Finally, Cassems took Liz Brandy to the door, holding her hand. He smiled weakly as she stepped over the threshold. Touched one of the floppy wings and let his hand drop.

Perhaps she knew.

He thought she did.

At the little bridge she turned and smiled gently. She was that enigma again.

He closed his eyes and when he opened them after a few seconds, she was gone.

CHAPTER 32

Why Things Are

At the base of the cliff Liz looked up from her feet, stained
from the damp soil as she had walked slowly back down the
path, pretending fitfully, to be carefree. Marty and Denny
stood waiting. Anxious, afraid they had trespassed, afraid for
some reason beyond their understanding that they may have
lost their Liz. Too afraid not to follow yet scared that it was
the wrong thing to do.

She stopped and stared at these men in her life. For a while
only the wind moved. They did not ask about the costume or
the trip. They never would.

Liz began to cry. It was a cry that farewelled a part of her life
and moved her onward. She walked to the boys and knelt
down and held them tighter than she had ever held onto

anything before. Her crying was infectious. They started to cry with no idea why. It seemed the right thing to be doing. An odd little shaking group.

A seabird hovered above. Out of sight it watched these creatures. It knew a little of their habits, handed down by collective memory. They run, they move in and out of the water, they lay still.
Now they are digging in the sand again.

It will be the last time.

Leo Cassems
Diary note
I am doing the cruellest thing it is possible to do.
I am throwing away friendship and love.
I need these visions to remain intact. They're too powerful.
I am selfish beyond even my belief?
I need an accomplice. Perhaps it is the fault of time.
That damned, unstoppable plough that pushes us onward.
If time could be purchased and packed away then there would
be no need for my actions. This last year could sit proudly on
my shelf, leather bound and gold blocked, available at any
time in the future to be taken down and rediscovered.
If I stay then it will all change.

As it is, the night has fallen and the girl has gone. And it must be forever.

This page is all about me. My wants, my needs.

Should I be more considerate? God, I hate myself.

No dammit. There's a greater good. How many people have what I have and would let it go in order to be left with only the faint essence of its creation.

I want to archive time.

CHAPTER 33

When There Is No End

DIARY NOTE - Elizabeth Brandy February - Summer -

Here it is again. A memory. A report. One of his paintings
sold for a record amount. Photo of Leo and Deborah Cassems
with their children and their dog Milo. They are with architect
Morris Yates and his wife and children.
All looking so tanned and relaxed. They're on his back deck.
The painting is reproduced in colour across the whole
page of the newspaper with much praise in the text from a
journalist called Bennett. There are my brothers and me on
our haunches, hidden in the black shadow of undergrowth, a
mass of tropical green, we are staring up into the tree canopy
with just enough light on our faces to be noticeable. As if we
are part of landscape. Just as he wanted us. It was the trip to
Morris Pools.

Once again the famous 'Hole' painting from the National Gallery is there as well with the three of us curled in its depths. He was right.

I am in my university cafe, under the trees, waiting for Marty and Denny to get out of their lectures. We're glued together tighter than .... I remember he searched for words before settling on "a palm trunk." Odd but apt.

Nobody ever asked, ever imagined. The works have become icons and we are cowered, waiting for the knock at the door and the flashes of light and the exposure. Perhaps we secretly wanted it at first. Those that knew, those few, have remained decent and loyal to the secret.

We're Cassems' inventions. And he has left it that way.

I need finality. Did I know we'd never meet again when I walked down his path?

He wanted us to stay the same and the only way to achieve his wish was to cut us off forever.

I went to The Dancing Frog once in case he was there. I wanted to see him, to tell him.

I understand but I hate him for it. Jenn and Tom just 'understand.' Which is rubbish.

After they received his letter and sold the beach house.

How could that be simple 'understanding.' I've seen them looking at the painting he gave us. I know he broke something more than trust.

I can't stay sad forever.

Do it now! Do it now!

I'll keep these words but close the book.

Goodbye.

It ends with the turn of a page. The writing on the page is
neat. There is the drawing of a seashell and another of a bird.
Open any page and it is all still there. In golden lines, it has
been set down and will not change.
So it was and will ever be.